Creative Scripts
for
Hypnotherapy

CREATIVE
SCRIPTS
FOR
HYPNOTHERAPY

Marlene E. Hunter, M.D.

BRUNNER/MAZEL, *Publishers* • NEW YORK

Library of Congress Cataloging-in-Publication Data

Hunter, Marlene E. (Marlene Elva)
    Creative scripts for hypnotherapy / Marlene E. Hunter.
        p.   cm.
    New and rev. ed. of: Daydreams for discovery.
    Includes bibliographical references.
    ISBN 0-87630-742-X :
    1. Hypnotism—Therapeutic use.   I. Hunter, Marlene E. (Marlene
Elva),   Daydreams for discovery.   II. Title.
    RC495.H86   1994
    616.89'162—dc20   94-6138
                                                               CIP

New and revised edition of *Daydreams for Discovery: A Manual for Hypnotherapists,*
originally copyrighted © Canada 1988 by SeaWalk Press Ltd.

Published by
BRUNNER/MAZEL, INC.
19 UNION SQUARE WEST
NEW YORK, NEW YORK 10003

MANUFACTURED IN THE UNITED STATES OF AMERICA

10 9 8 7 6 5 4 3 2

for many dear and wonderful friends

and especially to the memory of
Michael John Chamberlain Crooks
1930–1992

Contents

Part VIII: Sexuality

Part IX: Rehabilitation

Preface

This manual is still, as I said in the foreword to the first edition, *Daydreams for Discovery: A Manual for Hypnotherapists,* basically a collection of some of my favorite techniques and approaches that use hypnosis to bring relief for a wide variety of distressing situations.

However, it has been expanded considerably. There are updates on the current state-of-the-art with regard to research in various areas, there is a greatly expanded reference and bibliography section, and there are more case histories and increased discussion of when one might use a certain script or type of script.

The scripts are still meant to be spoken aloud. If they are merely read silently, they lose most of their impact. They are presented as I have spoken them many, many times in more than 20 years of doing clinical hypnosis, both as an inherent part of my office practice when I was in Family Practice and in a referral practice. Since the first edition came out, I have gone into a full-time consulting practice because the need for this type of approach has been increasing by leaps and bounds. Patients and clients are becoming more aware; they know that we are not disconnected at the neck and they want guidance and tools by which they can be part of their own recovery.

When you are adapting the scripts for your own use, explore all the vocal inflections, the softness or loudness, the whispered emphasis and cadence and rhythms that bring your own personal flavor to your therapeutic interventions.

And, again, plagiarize like mad. In the same way that I have taken the words of my mentors in the past and converted them to make them personal for me, I invite you to do the same. I am still repaying those who have gone before, who have taught and shared their skills and experience and expertise with me. Sharing these with you helps me to repay that debt.

In turn, teach and share with those who follow us now; help to educate our colleagues to the fact that we all use hypnosis all the time, whether intentionally or otherwise, so it behooves us to learn what it's all about and use it wisely.

And—ENJOY!!

Marlene Hunter
June 1994

Acknowledgments

Again I wish to acknowledge the support of my colleagues who nagged, prodded, and wheedled me into putting together the first edition of this manual, as I certainly would not otherwise be writing this page for the second edition.

I owe a debt of gratitude, also, to the members of the American Society of Clinical Hypnosis for their encouragement in the form of electing me to the presidency of that organization, and continuing to ask me to serve on their teaching faculty for regional and annual workshops. Every time we teach, we learn.

And, always, special appreciation to my family—including those now in memoriam—for their support and encouragement all through my life.

PART I

THE BASIC BASICS

Induction Techniques
Self-Hypnosis Techniques
"Homework"
Literature and Commentary

1

Induction Techniques

There are surely as many induction techniques in hypnosis as there are people who practice hypnosis—indeed, many times that number, for almost everyone has several—and it would obviously be impossible even to describe all the main categories. I am going to give examples in this chapter of only three types—Basic Technique, Visual Imagery and Eye-Fixation—and then some hints for reducing resistance, to get you started if you are just beginning or to offer some new verbiage if you feel yours is getting stale or boring (even to yourself!!).

Just as important as WHAT you say is HOW you say it. I think that most of us fall into a sort of low drone, when we are doing inductions, which may or may not be the best way to lead someone into hypnosis. Probably, we do best when we are ourselves comfortable with how softly we are speaking, and with the cadence of our words, whatever those might be. I knew one highly successful hypnotherapist whose words ran together into a sort of staccato gobbledegook, with scarely a pause for breath, that one would have thought would discourage the most dedicated subject; yet it worked well for him, simply because he presumed that it would. And that master of hypnosis, Milton Erickson, was very hard to understand in the last few months (or even years) of his life, and yet his success with patients was inevitable both because HE was confident and because he inspired that confidence in all who came to him.

However, I do think there are a few basic "rules" that help to smooth the way. One is to make sure that your words and the tone of your voice are compatible. Inviting someone to go deeper and deeper and deeper will be less effective than making sure that your voice falls with each repetition of the word "deeper." The subconscious implication, the nonverbal message, is always more imperative than mere words.

Another important point is to avoid, at all costs, phrasing your suggestions in the negative mode. "You will not feel panicky" will almost surely invite panic. "You can feel very comfortable" or ". . .very much at ease" has a much greater chance of success. Even the most experienced of us tend to forget, at times, that the language of the subconscious is imagery (words and logic belong to the language of the conscious mind) and it is very, very difficult to have a negative image. Please do not think of a pink elephant. Right?

Use permissive, comfortable words; we are *inviting* people into hypnosis. "Let yourself feel as relaxed as you wish to feel at this time...," "You may find it interesting to go exploring. . . ."

Eschew—vigorously—that most sabotaging word in the English language: TRY. "Trying" always allows, in the back of the mind, for the possibility of failure. There are many things one can do rather than "try." One can search, learn, discover, find out more about, explore (I like that one best)—and all of these have a much more positive connotation than "trying," which all too often makes one weary just thinking about it. (Or, of course, one can just DO it, which is the best one of all.)

Remember that there is nothing wrong with a few minutes of silence every now and then, or a gentle, reassuring murmur: "Um-hum, Um-hum" or "*That's* right." My friend Dr. Claire Frederick calls these "comforting noises." I use them all the time, as you will discover throughout this book.

We must also pay attention, when appropriate, to culture. In general, the approach to hypnosis in North America is very permissive. This is not necessarily so in other cultures: the Europeans may tend to be more formal, more authoritarian, and hypnosis as it is practiced in African or other cultures very different from ours will include many allusions and perhaps even rituals which seem alien to us. We must be very aware of these differences, for "trying" to lead someone into hypnosis will be an exercise in futility for all concerned if we ignore such fundamental issues. This also applies to working with North American native Indians, who are very proud of their heritage. It is easy, and it will not be taken amiss, to ask, "What type of entry into hypnosis will be most comfortable for you?"

For that matter, many practitioners do not use formal inductions any more. They may not even specify that they prefer their patients/clients to close their eyes. Instead, phrases such as "Just settle down comfortably—that's right," with or without some comment about listening or letting the conscious mind go off to do its own thing, is all the "induction" there is.

Personally, I usually still use a simple induction, especially if the person is a novice. It is comforting, and makes him/her feel taken care of, setting the scene and meeting the client's expectations.

A word about hypnotizability. There are several well-known Scales of Hypnotizability—the Spiegel (described in *Trance and Treatment*, 1987), Stanford (Weitzenhoffer & Hilgard, 1962) and Harvard (Shor & Orne, 1962) scales are the best known. There is one area where the use of such scales is important: research.

In research, one wants to narrow the variables as much as possible. One way to achieve the most consistent results is to choose participants who fit into a certain level of hypnotizability as defined by these various measuring techniques.

Clinically, however, I am of the opinion that MOTIVATION is the most important factor, while the ability to go more or less deeply into hypnosis is secondary. There is a great deal of anecdotal material in the literature about this. Especially interesting is a seminal article by Barber (1977) about the use of hypnotic pain relief techniques in "unhypnotizable" subjects. Those of us who have been practicing hypnosis for several years all have our own experiences in this regard.

However, many practitioners feel more comfortable using the hypnotizability criteria; for them, that is, of course, the best thing to do.

When all is said and done, I come right back to my earlier comments: be comfortable yourself, and you will have a more comfortable subject.

BASIC INDUCTION TECHNIQUE

Settle yourself down into a very comfortable position. That's right. Remember, you can always move or shift your position any time, to make yourself more comfortable. Make sure your back and head are supported, and everything feels just right.

reassuring that the subject has control

physical comfort is important

Now let your eyes find something pleasant and convenient to focus on and just keep looking at that, whatever it might be, for a little time.

By and by you may find your eyes getting just a little heavier and it seems as if it would be nice to let them close for a little while. Find out how it feels to let them close for a few seconds and then open them again — then close open one more time and close — that's right. You may notice that there is a gentle flickering in your eyelids. That can be a cue for you, that you are entering some delightful space in your mind where time loses its usual meaning and you are able to perceive so many things in a different way.

less intimidating than the suggestion to close them — period — especially in an inexperienced subject

if you watch carefully, you will see the eyes glaze just before they flicker — a good time to mention it!

Imagine yourself in some very nice place, where everything is just the way it would be if you could order it specially for yourself. And as you spend a little time there, gradually the tightness eases away and you become even more comfortable.

makes it personal

acknowledges the tightness (i.e., tension) which most inexperienced subjects have

Fill in all the details of your daydream: what you might see in your mind's eye, and what you might hear with your inward ear; how your body feels with whatever it is doing in your imagination. If you are lying on a tropical beach, feel the warm sun, feel the sand, feel the movement in your body as it snuggles down into a comfortable position in the sand. If you are swimming in that tropical lagoon, feel the movement in your body as it glides through the water, feel the water as it slips coolly over your skin. Find out how your body *feels*.

"inward" **differentiated from** *"outward"*

invoke *all* **the senses: visual, auditory, kinesthetic, touch, smell, taste, warmth/coolness**

There may be things in your daydream that you want to reach out and touch, or taste. There may be aromas that are associated with that. Find out what the colors are like, whether it is warm or cool, if there's anyone else there — all the details that add color and richness and enjoyment to our daydreaming.

implying comfortably that we all daydream and this is so similar

And while you are doing that, your inner mind will be taking you to your own best level of comfortable hypnosis, whatever is just right for you, to achieve what you are going to achieve today.

whatever YOU (the subject) do, is right

VISUAL IMAGERY

(Remember that many people do not visualize and this technique would be frustrating rather than enjoyable)

Settle back very comfortably in your chair, let
your eyes close, and imagine your favorite big
white fluffy cloud settling down beside you —
so close that you can climb on to that cloud
and embark on a wonderful fantasy.

the invitation

Feel the fluffiness and soft supportiveness of
that cloud, as it gently envelops you and
begins to lift you up, so that you are floating,
floating up into the sky completely protected,
comfortably supported, absolutely safe.

**kinesthetic awareness
added to visual imagery**

essential to feel SAFE

As the cloud drifts easily through the sky, an
inquisitive bird swoops down and lands beside
you on the cloud. It looks at you questioningly
as if to say, "Come, play tag with me!"

**(you may wish to make
sure that there are no
bird phobias)**

Then it spreads its wings and takes off again,
dipping and swooping and soaring around the
cloud, getting caught on a warm updraught of
air, wafted on a soft breeze, completely free.

Your cloud seems to want to follow the bird,
and you, too, are wondering where it might
lead you. Below, you can see the tops of the
trees and yet amazingly, from your place on
the cloud, you can also see every branch and
leaf outlined in delicate tracery; the green
and yellow fields of grain have wind-waves
skittering across them and there is the silver
ribbon of a little river winding its way
through the valley.

be inquisitive

And then you glimpse, off in the distance, a
rainbow — clear, arched high in the heavens.
The bird seems to have sensed it also, and to
be flying towards it.

**(not useful for people who
are color blind)**

As you come closer, you marvel at the effer-
vescent colors of that rainbow. Each color

seems somehow to be shaded with silver so
that it is pure and translucent and almost
gleaming, yet soft, soft—unlike any colors
you have ever seen.

*each person will have his/
her own ideas of what
these colors are like*

The bird leads you into a mother-of-pearl
pink, the delicate shell-like glow of early
dawn. It seems to you as if you are being
offered a new awakening. The color
surrounds you and your cloud reflects
the pastel tones.

**"a new awakening" is very
suggestive for change**

The pearly color leads into a soft golden
orange, the way the sky glows just before
the sun comes up. It brings with it the
promise of the sun's warm healing and
you bask in that wonderful color, feeling
that healing begin within you.

**promise of good things to
come**

**the sun is often a symbol
of healing — *"healing begin"*
is part of the promise, part
of the new awakening**

Now you follow the little bird as it leads
you into the soft green shade, the verdant
symbol of growth and renewal. It is such a
wonderful color, full of possibilities—the
color of spring, of tender new plants, of leaf
buds bursting from the grey branches of
winter and bringing new life. This is the
color we all wait for as the bleak dark days
of winter start to lengthen and to lighten
into new promise.

**growth and renewal
further the metaphor**

"new promise" **reiterates
previous phrases**

And from there, into the clear blue of the
heavens and is it your imagination or does the
bird particularly enjoy that color? With the
blue comes calmness and serenity, coolness
and comfort.

symbol of acceptance

Gradually, the blue transmutes into the
soft purple of the evening sky—a time for
contemplation, for re-viewing, for gaining a
new sense of oneself in the Universe.

re-view: **to see again, a new
perspective**

The bird, its feathers iridescent, frolics
in and out between the colors of the
rainbow, as if beckoning to you and
saying, "Come, you too can be part of
this whole Universe."

you are not alone

(Silence, for a little time)

And now you know, somehow, that it is
time to go home again — to drift and float
with the cloud, back to that place where you
began this journey. The bird follows you
again, dipping and swooping around,
beckoning you to play, but you know that
the time for that is finished for a little while,
and for now the cloud will take you back
home safely, settling you into your chair,
into yourself, and you can join the bird
again another day.

more possibilities await

EYE FIXATION TECHNIQUE

Just settle yourself comfortably in the chair,
put your feet up on the footstool — that's right.
Do you have any questions, just before we
start? No? Fine.

opportunity to participate

Then just look at my thumb, which I am
slowly going to bring closer and closer to
your forehead. And of course, if you look
at anything with your eyes backwards long
enough, your eyes begin to get a little tired
and you feel like closing them. So there's
nothing magical about that, either. The only
difference is that this time, when you close
them, it will be a signal, to yourself and to
me, that you are ready to go into some level
of hypnosis — whatever is just right and
comfortable for you today.

**hold your hand about
30 cm. above the forehead,
with the fingers *very* lightly
flexed; a fist, or an open
hand, can appear
threatening. Bring the
thumb slowly to rest
between the eyebrows**

**stating the implicit
contract**

So just keep staring at my thumb — that's right — and you may notice that the eyes are beginning to moisten a little bit. . .and soon the lids will begin to flicker. . .that's right — yes, just let them close gently, and imagine yourself in some very nice place, where everything is just the way it would be if you could choose it especially for yourself.

the eyes always moisten at this stage — and the lids flicker

eyes close — contract accepted

personal place

That little flicker you feel in your eyelids is probably the most common thing that happens when people are just beginning to go into hypnosi, and it happpens because of the position the eyes rest in, as we go into hypnosis.

validating the trance experience

Later on, when you learn to do your own hypnosis, you can use it as a signal for yourself — that you are just ready to go into that very pleasant state. Some people find that it will persist; for others, it eases away quite quickly; for many, it seems to come and go, probably depending on changing levels in hypnosis, but it's almost always there to begin with. So you can think of it as a nice clue, that you are just entering that very pleasant state.

this is *your* tool

whatever happens, is the right thing to happen

(Now begin your therapeutic program for the day)

Variations on this Technique

1. The subject holds a pen or pencil at arm's length and uses that as a focusing point.
2. Or invite him/her to fix on some point on the opposite wall, or on some object in the room.
3. Some people use a candle or a softly lit lamp.

HINTS FOR REDUCING RESISTANCE

Resistance is a perfectly normal — and even admirable — quality which is found in virtually all novice subjects, but also is frequently present in subjects who are very experienced, especially if they are about to explore unknown or muddy waters in their hypnosis. It is simply a reflection of the subconscious doing its protective work.

Prime examples of this can be found in survivors of child abuse who have used dissociation to survive the abuse. They are masters at hypnosis, but are at times extremely reluctant to go into hypnosis because they know—whether consciously or not—the dragons that lie in the deep and murky waters of the mind. We must respect that subconscious protection. They will use hypnosis, formally or not, when they are ready to do so.

The first opportunity to defuse resistance comes when you are explaining to inexperienced subjects about hypnosis in general, remarking that resistance is normal and even to be desired. It is a signal that their wise, deep, inner mind is taking care of them. That is why most people are very light hypnotic subjects to begin with, and then go further into hypnosis when they have realized that they have been there many times before but may have called it "daydreaming" or "being lost in thought."

The preamble is also a good time to implant positive suggestions such as "I can see that you are well motivated, and that is *the* most important quality for a successful hypnotic experience."

Many people will state, rather belligerently, "I can NEVER relax!" The response to that is to say, quickly, "Oh, please DO NOT relax! Simply enjoy listening to my voice. You are one of those people who will do their best work when they are *listening closely,* and *focus*ing on what I am saying." We know that the subconscious mind tends to disregard the negatives and "please DO NOT . . ." will be interpreted as "please DO. . . ."

With appropriate voice inflection, there are further suggestions to "listen closely" and "focus"—admirable hypnotic directives.

For those subjects who keep their eyes open, the happy comment, "Oh, you are one of those people who like to *go into hypnosis with your eyes open*. . ." will usually result in an immediate closing of the eyes.

You will find it worthwhile to spend a little time finding out about the person's preferred imagery and—even more important—about any fears or phobias. Someone who is afraid of water will certainly resist the suggestion to go canoeing in his/her imagination.

Find out about previous hypnotic experiences, especially stage hypnosis. Negative impressions may need to be discussed, and reassurance given that clinical hypnosis is very different from entertainment hypnosis and that you know your job.

State and restate several times that whatever happens is the right thing to happen at any hypnotic experience. Tell everybody that most people are very light subjects when they are just beginning, and will learn to go more deeply when they become somewhat more familiar with the techniques.

If your subject is *very* resistant, you may want to request earnestly, "Please, only go into hypnosis with your *subconscious* mind, and keep your conscious mind apart." This is a double whammy because of the implications of dissociation.

Remember what has been stated before — we are *inviting* people into hypnosis, not propelling them against their will. Humankind seems to have a natural rebellion against being TOLD to do something; we tend to reply (often subconsciously, of course), "I don't *want* to do that — and *you can't make me!*" The child within us is exercising his or her prerogative to be as obstructive as possible. Use a soft inviting voice, even if the direction is a command disguised as an invitation. Words such as "let" and "may" ("Let your subconscious mind . . ." or "You may find it interesting to . . .") will reassure the person that, in hypnosis, the decision to explore or to go more deeply into hypnosis belongs to the subject. Our task is to lead, never to push or drag. And never, NEVER to imply by words or actions (or body language) that the subject is in any way to "blame" for not having a "good enough" experience of hypnosis. "What happens, is the right thing to happen for you, at this time."

2

Self-Hypnosis Techniques

TEACHING SELF-HYPNOSIS

It is time for you to begin doing your own hypnosis at home, to strengthen and reinforce what we do here. And in order to do that, you will need to arrange, with yourself, your own personal self-hypnosis approach — some little pattern or pathway or routine or formula that you can use, that you can feel very comfortable with, to take yourself into hypnosis. As you know, everybody experiences hypnosis in their own way. It is very, very personal. But there are some general patterns that are common.

concept of cooperative, joint project

In the same way, we each have our own, very personal, self-hypnosis approach; but there are some general patterns that are common there also. It is some of these general patterns that I'm going to describe for you now. As I describe them, perhaps one of the ones that I mention will seem just right for you — with some little modification to suit you specially: a different word, perhaps, or a different phrase; a different memory or image than the one that I might suggest; maybe a different rhythm or cadence as you think of the words; or maybe even a different language than the one that I am

personalizing the technique

use when English is a second language

13

using, because it can be very comforting to go back to the language of one's own childhood. Or perhaps something that I say will remind you of something in your own experience that you would like to adapt as a self-hypnosis approach. So that in one of those ways you will arrange, with yourself, for your own special self-hypnosis technique.

remembering past experience is an altered state (regression)

Keep it simple. In hypnosis, the best techniques are always very simple; so just keep it simple and easy and comfortable — and one of the simplest routines, that is very commonly used, is just to count yourself down. People who use that technique get into a comfortable position, reclining or sitting down with the head supported (that's very important, for the sake of comfort), close their eyes with the intention of going into hypnosis and simply . . . count. Some people just continue to count slowly and steadily till they reach the level that's just right for them at that time; others have already arranged with themselves about that. They may have said, "When I reach '15,' I'll be in a light hypnosis; when I reach '20,' I'll be in a medium hypnosis; when I reach '25,' I can work on this project" — that sort of thing. Some people like to recite a little series of numbers over and over: "1--2-- 3--4--5, 1--2--3---4----5, 1---2----3----- 4-----5--." Some people like to recite the alphabet instead of counting. That's kind of fun — it reminds us of one of our earliest achievements: learning the alphabet — the symbol of all those grown-up things like books and letters and newspapers and things like that.

avoid the idea of lying down as it suggests sleep instead of hypnosis

"project" has a more positive connotation than "problem"

invitation for regression childhood — a hypnotic suggestion

A variation of those, but really the same thing, is to see yourself or FEEL yourself going down a beautiful stairway, or perhaps a terraced garden (or climbing a Stairway to the Stars,

many people have kinesthetic, rather than visual, imagery

floating from one step up to the next), where each step, each terrace takes you one level further into hypnosis, and you can take as many steps, as many terraces as are just right for you at that particular time. These are the straightforward, direct pathways into hypnosis—very simple, very easy, very commonly used, and very useful.

people who feel like they are floating into hypnosis may find it incongruous to float "down;" also, the concept of going down or deeper is disturbing to some; offer a choice—to go *up* the stairs, to go *further* into hypnosis

Some people prefer more imagery. They might like to imagine themselves drifting down a beautiful little river in a small canoe, the sun dappling through the leaves and sparkling on the water, the soft sound and movement of the water carrying them gently into hypnosis. Or floating on a cloud, or going out to explore the galaxies, or just having their very favorite daydream. Some people use color. If you close your eyes and see a lovely kaleidoscope of color across your inner vision, you might like to adapt that as a self-hypnosis technique; or seeing a pinpoint of color way off in the distance, and as you watch it, it comes closer; and so you watch it and it comes closer and closer and gets bigger and bigger, and comes closer and gets bigger until you are enveloped in that gorgeous color; and the color takes you into hypnosis.

check about fear of water *before* using this suggestion

Some people prefer the comfortable, familiar things: the ticking of a clock; the sound of waves on a beach; a favorite piece of music; or perhaps the rhythm of their own breathing—or even the memory of my thumb, as it comes softly down to touch their forehead.*

inward focusing on breathing

tends to deepen hypnosis (inward focusing is one attribute of the altered state)

(*my usual office induction)

Choose for yourself, now, some little pattern that is just right for YOU, and really focus on that for a few minutes. Go over it several times in your mind. Imagine yourself taking yourself

reinforcement

into hypnosis, using that approach. Think about getting ready to do your hypnosis, taking yourself in imagination to the place where you are going to be doing that; settle yourself down (with head supported, remember, that's very important); close the eyes with the intention of going into hypnosis. Feel that little flicker in your eyelids as you take yourself in with your *own* induction, and enjoy your hypnosis within your hypnosis. Just rehearse that whole scenario. That's right; that's right.

"imagine yourself taking yourself. . ." hypnotic language

substituting self- for hetero-induction

"hypnosis within your hypnosis" — a double inductive and powerful deepening suggestion

We're going to establish that as your own personal pattern in this way: I'll begin to count you out, but before I reach "1," you'll feel my thumb, and when you feel that, using your *own* technique take yourself back down again, a little further than where you are now, just a little: 5--4--easy now--3--halfway there-- 2 *(touching forehead with my thumb)* — and now taking yourself back down in your own way, my thumb just a reinforcer for your own special self-hypnosis approach. That's right — just a *little* deeper than you were before. Good.

strong suggestion for feeling in control of their own trance
"deeper" seems more acceptable after establishing the concept of "further"

Now, think about that for a few moments, and find out if that is exactly the way you want your own technique to go. If you want to make any changes, arrange those with yourself now. That's right.

opportunity to rehearse again in a slightly different way

We're going to reinforce it now in a similar way. I'll begin to count you out, but before I reach "1" you'll feel my thumb again — when you feel it, using your *own* technique, take yourself back down again, yet a little further than where you are now — just a little bit: 5--- 4---3-- *(touching forehead)* and down again now, taking yourself back in your own way, my thumb just a reinforcer, that's all — just a

downplaying the therapist's role in the subject's hypnosis, continuing strong positive suggestions for knowing *they* are in control and approval for doing it "right"

reinforcer for your own special way of taking yourself into hypnosis. Just ease in comfortably to that deeper level, wherever it is just right for you at this time. That's right—very nice, indeed.

Now, you've done several things, just since you've been here this afternoon. You have arranged, and you have established, AND you've reinforced your own self-hypnosis approach—*AND* you have also learned a deepening technique, one that we call "fractionating": that is, going a little way into hypnosis and then coming part way out, a fraction of the way out, then going a little further than you were to begin with, then part way out from there, then going still further, and so on. This is a very easy little technique that you might use when for some reason you would like to ease more deeply into hypnosis. As you know, we can never force the subconscious to do anything; we can certainly never force it to go more deeply into hypnosis—but we can always *encourage*, yes, we can encourage, and that's what these deepening techniques are all about: ways to encourage a deeper level of hypnosis when you think it would be more comfortable, or more useful, or more appropriate, or just more fun, to do that.

We find that when people are first beginning to do their own hypnosis, there is really only one important thing, and that is to do it at least once every day. This means setting aside a specific time designated as hypnosis time. You know, it is often a temptation to think, "Oh, I'll do it when I finish these other things," or "I'll do it at the end of this project," or something like that. Uh-uh. Uh-uh. You shortchange yourself that way. Rather than that, set aside a specific time, *prearranged,*

to impress on them, their several achievements

interpreting the term "fraction-ating"

many options and opportunities

post-hypnotic suggestion for practicing regularly

label that as "hypnosis time," and that is the
time when you do your hypnosis. You have
an appointment with yourself at that time; it
is probably the most important appointment
that you will have all day. Some people prefer,
for example, to always do their hypnosis at 4
o'clock; some like to arrange it when they get
up in the morning and look at their daily
schedule, some decide the night before —
do it however it works best for you, but DO
prearrange it because that way, you'll be
giving it the special attention that it deserves.

nobody likes to be short-changed, and it avoids the word "not," which the sub-conscious tends to ignore (thus creating the opposite suggestion to what was intended)

ego-strengthening

ego-strengthening and positive attributes of self-hypnosis

Now, maybe it's a very busy day and you
feel you only have five minutes; that's fine —
take five minutes. Maybe it's a more leisurely
day and you have fifteen minutes. Fine; take
fifteen minutes. The length of time is much
less important. The important thing — the
only really vital thing — is to do it at least once
every day. Because hypnosis is a conditioned
response. The more you do it, the better you
get at it. The better you get at it, the more
useful it becomes. The more useful it becomes,
the more you want to do it, and the more you
do it, the better you get at it; so very quickly
you get into a very, very positive feedback
cycle. And, you know, everybody deserves
at least five minutes of their own time every
day. You do. You've earned that time. So
take that time for your own hypnosis and
enjoy it. Yes. Make that commitment to
yourself right at this time — to do your
hypnosis at least once, every day.

permission to choose own time length and also a way to gently forestall excuses

ego-strengthening

After all, hypnosis is a talent that comes from
within you. It is part of your own rich inner
resources. And learning more about it, how to
access it and use it, can bring you reward and
satisfaction, all through your life.

reinforcing sense of self-control and inner strengths

GENERAL COMMENTS

Chatting for a few minutes to your subjects about the general principles of self-hypnosis will be time well spent. Otherwise they may come back at the next visit very discouraged and say, "It just didn't work at all!"

What they mean is, "It wasn't the same as it is here with you doing the induction."

Forewarning them about this may prevent some of the disillusionment. I usually explain that self-hypnosis is seldom as deep as hetero-hypnosis, especially when people are just beginning. My rationale is that when we are doing self-hypnosis, we keep one little part of the conscious mind alert, "to do the guiding," whereas in hetero-hypnosis that little corner can also "relax into hypnosis." This explanation usually has a favorable reception. I go on to say that sometimes they may surprise themselves, and come out of their self-hypnosis wondering where they have been for the past half-hour, but that these episodes happen *spontaneously,* and never because we demand that they happen.

Reiterate that if they have a very light and perhaps therefore disappointing session, it is still worthwhile because EVERY experience will reinforce the technique; and furthermore, the aggravating fact is that the subconscious will determine the level of hypnosis and there isn't much that we can do about that, except "encourage" a deeper level with some of the simple deepening techniques such as fractionation.

Teach your subject about the importance of phrasing, the avoidance of "not" words, and how to do simple affirmations (see the section on Ego-Strengthening). Suggest that they limit their agenda to one or two items for each session. Some people get a great deal of benefit out of speaking the message(s) thay they wish to give to themselves into a tape recorder and then playing the tape while they are in self-hypnosis. Listening to one's own voice while in hypnosis is a very powerful technique and your subject will appreciate that suggestion.

I always emphasize that we can do great work in just a few minutes, if that is all the time we have on any particular day. (Of course there is almost always a way to find more time, but people think that they have too much else to do.) Reiterate that everyone deserves a few minutes of their own time, each day. This discourages the excuse, "I just didn't have time."

Urge them to STOP *"TRYING"*!!

Remind them of the eyelid flutter that they will now be aware of, and that they can use that in their own hypnosis as an indication of their readiness to go further into hypnosis.

Reassure them that "simple messages are best," and that you KNOW they can do it!

3

"Homework"

As I described earlier, in my practice I usually spend the first two or three sessions with new and/or inexperienced hypnosis patients teaching them the basic tools of hypnosis—simple relaxation techniques, some problem-solving methods, and self-hypnosis. I explain that unless people can use these basic tools, they compromise their chances of getting the very best out of their hypnosis.

Nobody wants to compromise his/her chances, so virtually every patient nods acquiescence when I tell them this.

Nevertheless, people want SOME acknowledgement that you know why they are there and what their main concerns are, so I devised a general and very simple way to accomplish this: near the end of the first and second sessions, "Now, it's time to give the subconscious some homework."

I use the scripts that follow in 90% of cases, and every subject immediately translates the scripts as being devised for him/her personally. It brings a high degree of satisfaction—and, very often, interesting things happen, which the client then tells me about at the next session.

Further on in therapy, you may wish to suggest some very specific "homework" assignments, but that is a different matter. Such assignments are also extremely useful, and increase the sense of participation on the part of the patient.

"HOMEWORK"—FIRST SESSION

It's time now for me to speak more directly to the subconscious *(beginning to turn head so that your voice is coming from a different direction);* so let your conscious mind do whatever it wants to do. It can listen, if it wants—and probably it will, because the conscious mind is always very curious about what's going on — it always wants to *know* things; so probably it will want to listen. However, it may want to go off on a daydream of its own, or have its attention diverted by this or that, or organize something for tomorrow — that's fine, just let it go. I'm now speaking to the SUBCONSCIOUS, because it's time to give the subconscious some homework.

this obviates any anxiety about the mind wandering, that they are "not doing it right"

There are two homework assignments for the subconscious today.

The first, is to go exploring for you; to go searching — through the past, yes, and through the present — perhaps even through the future, searching for information that could be useful for you, as we continue with these sessions.

dissociative, crossing time spans; "exploring... through the future" is also a confusion technique. This also gives the message that useful information is gathered throughout one's lifetime, which can be adapted when we need it

Your subconscious will gather up this information, sift it, filter it, organize it — get it ready to present to your conscious awareness at appropriate times, and in very appropriate ways.

You will probably not be very aware of this going on. Usually the subconscious continues to work at a SUB-conscious level, at this stage. But from time to time you may get a little glimpse or glimmer: an old memory might come into your mind — you might wonder why on earth you're thinking of *that,* right then; or something that has always seemed a little confused around the edges — although you don't exactly know why — may somehow seem clearer — although you don't exactly know how; or you may find yourself thinking about something you've thought about dozens of times before, but somehow you're thinking about it from a slightly different angle — as if you've moved over one notch — and that might be helpful in

if the subconscious chooses to ignore this "not," so much the better

reassurance that "you'll know about it in time"

patients often report at the next session, "I've been remembering the oddest things!"

suggesting spontaneous reframing

some way, you might wonder why you hadn't thought of it that way before.

But if these things happen, I think you'll find that they happen at a very, very subtle level — just little glimpses into the work that your subconscious has been doing for you.

suggestions for accepting "nothing happening"

The second assignment is similar, and may be done simultaneously: and that is, to allow your subconscious to begin to reevaluate old things from the past that are interfering with the present.

this is really a suggestion for reframing

You know, the little girl (boy) looks at a house, and it seems so big; the tree in the front yard is so tall, and the hill behind the house so steep. But if that little girl (boy) goes back many years later, then the woman (man) that s/he has become finds the house to be quite an ordinary house, really. It might even seem a bit on the small side. And it's a nice enough tree, but it's just an ordinary tree; and the hill behind the house seems somehow to be a gentler slope.

simple example that almost everyone can identify

And the house, and the tree, and the hill haven't changed — but *s/he* has. All of those experiences, as you know, were absolutely real; all of those interpretations were absolutely valid. They were simply *different,* because the situation of the person was different.

validating *both* the child's and the adult's views, and that the reality of the child is different from the reality of the adult but equally valid

In the same way, it is quite alright to allow your subconscious to reevaluate old things from the past, *perfectly valid when they began* and useful — maybe even necessary; but because we know that things that are valid and useful and necessary at one stage of our lives may not necessarily be valid or useful or necessary at another stage of our lives, then they deserve to be reassessed. Because maybe some of them have become obsolete, out of date. And if so, then it's time for them to be revised, resolved, modified, brought up to date, taken care of in some way, so that they can finally and completely be finished, and put away.

decisions and actions of the past *were* valid at the time (obviates blame and guilt)

new circumstances and information may change the picture

And in that way, it is as if you give yourself some space, for new, good things to happen.

suggestion that new good things *will* happen

(As you begin to close the session, gradually turn your head again so that your voice is coming from the original position.)

"HOMEWORK" — SECOND SESSION

Time now for me once again to speak more directly to the subconscious *(turning your head as you did in the previous session),* so let your conscious mind do whatever it wants to do; if it wants to listen, that's fine; or if it wants to go off on its own, that's fine, too. I'm speaking now directly to the subconscious, because once again it's time to give the subconscious some homework and once again, there are two homework assignments for the subconscious today.

reorienting back to a previous hypnotic experience is a deepening technique

You remember that last time, the first assignment was for your subconscious to go exploring for you, searching for information that could be useful for you as we continued with these sessions.

further reinforcement

This time, that part of the assignment is much more specific: and that is, that your subconscious mind *extracts,* from that great wealth of information that it has been

positive suggestions that the subconscious has done its work

gathering — extracts information that is
particularly relevant to some specific situation
that the subconscious chooses! We allow the
subconscious to choose the situation. Because,
you see, we may think we know — well, of
course, we DO know — some situation that
needs attention. But the subconscious has so
much more information than the conscious
mind has, the subconscious mind may know
of some situation that needs to be taken care
of, FIRST — and *then* it can go on and pay
attention to what the conscious mind thinks
is more important.

**important because the sub-
ject may otherwise presume
something "wrong" or "not
working"**
**reassuring that the therapist
remembers the original
task**
validating the suggestion

So we allow the subconscious to choose the
situation, to extract the information that
it needs relevant to that — and then to do
whatever it needs to do, to take care of that.

**simple statement covering
just about everything!**

So you're going to have an interesting week;
because something in your life is going to
change a little bit, in a positive way, and
we don't know what it is, yet.

**an exciting little mystery
to look forward to**

Oh, it will probably be something very
minor — just some little thing: something will
seem easier for you, it won't bother you so
much, you may think of a new way of doing
it — just some little thing that will smooth the
day to day pathway we all travel, to make
yours more comfortable for you.

**look for something good
and you will probably
find it**

Because it will probably just be something
very small, keep all your awarenesses open,
so that you are able to recognize that little
change, and so enjoy it.

reinforcement

The second assignment is the same as it
was before, and that is to allow your subconscious to begin to reevaluate old things

from the past, *perfectly valid when they began,* but which now may have become obsolete, out of date, and so deserve to be reassessed. Because maybe it IS time for one or some of them to be revised, resolved, modified, brought up to date, taken care of in some way—HEALED, perhaps—so that they can be finally and completely finished, and put away, and in that way you give yourself that space for the new, good things, *that are already happening!*—that's right, that are already happening.

the only new word in this suggestion is "HEALED": it is spoken with a pause just before it, to give it extra emphasis. This is a rather crucial time in therapy and the suggestion of "healing" is fervently received; and the patient is reassured that you remember why he/she came in the first place

(Close the session in a similar way to the first time, again moving your head back so that your voice is coming from the original direction)

ODDS 'n ENDS

What is the definition of a "problem"?
Answer: A problem is an opportunity to do something different!

And what is the definition of "frustration"?
Answer: Frustration is doing the same thing over and over and expecting a different result.

Useful phrases that I have picked up from somewhere, and that you can adapt to fit an incredible number of situations:

"You know more than you know that you know..."
(Erickson, via Hanley)

"Utilize something that you do well, to help you do something else, better..." (Rossi)

"You have the experience to learn what you need to know, and to know what you need to learn..." (Hunter, I think!)

4

Literature and Commentary

The whole field of hypnotic language and suggestopedia has evolved from the days when the "hypnotist" gave direct commands to the subject and expected those commands to be followed. If the subject was agreeable and comfortable with the situation, and was relatively unresistant at a moderately deep trance level, the expected could and often would happen.

But if there was resistance — conscious or unconscious — and the little rebel at the back of the mind said NO!, the hypnosis "failed."

Perhaps this is what happened to Freud, and the reason why he abandoned hypnosis as a therapeutic modality.

We are luckier today. People do research on the relative merits of direct versus indirect suggestion, the use of metaphor, whether scales of hypnotizability are important or unimportant in the clinical setting, and they ponder over what is called "the language of hypnosis."

There is some worthwhile literature on these subjects. Unfortunately, not all of it is easily accessible, because much of it has been presented at various conferences around the world, and may or may not be published in a book or journal that can be purchased on the open market.

One excellent publication is available, however, and that is the *Handbook of Hypnotic Suggestions and Metaphors* (Hammond, 1990). The section on "Formulating Hypnotic and Posthypnotic Suggestions" is an excellent overview of the subject.

Matheson and Shue (1989) presented an interesting paper at the Fourth European Congress of Hypnosis and Hypnotherapy held in Oxford and printed in the Proceedings of that meeting. They studied the experience of direct and indirect hypnosis in 50 subjects to see if either approach produced an overall increase in response or, if some persons responded better to the indirect and others to the direct approach.

As might have been expected, they discovered that some did better with the direct and others with the indirect approach; and they entered a plea for further study along this line, questioning whether or not this factor might play an even larger role than the Hypnotizability Scales in determining any particular subject's response to hypnotic intervention.

Evans (1989), at the same Congress, presented data suggesting that hypnotizability may be related to the ability to process cognitive information during sleep, and also to the physiological ease of falling asleep and wakening easily "on cue." This concept demands further study.

Many therapists who use hypnosis do feel that some form of assessing hypnotizability is useful clinically. For them, the best avenue still seems to be the various established scales, e.g., Spiegel or Stanford.

PART II

GETTING PAST ROADBLOCKS

Problem-Solving Techniques

Reframing

5

Problem-Solving Techniques

The patter that I use to introduce the topic of problem solving can be found on page 32, at the beginning of the script on The Three Boxes.

Problem solving in hypnosis offers an immediate opportunity "to do something different." People get so bogged down in their own dilemmas that they come to believe there is no relief and they can do nothing to escape. These techniques are simply new frameworks in which to review the situation. Deliberately fitting the problem into a structured approach often bemuses people and takes away some of the burden. The person no longer feels forced to create some sort of miracle "cure" for what probably involves several other people, too. The frustration of these situations is often centered around the wish that somehow the *other* people will change.

As a possible answer to the problem, such a hope is usually unrealistic.

Hypnosis brings the solution right back to the individual's doorstep in a much less threatening way, and the "gimmicks" that are offered allow a new approach. I will usually say, "There's nothing wrong with a good gimmick, as long as you know that it's a gimmick. In fact you can even laugh at yourself for using such a silly trick—but it still works!" And the patient laughs a little, too, and nods agreement.

There must be thousands of ways to approach problem solving in hypnosis. Most of them involve some way to turn blocks into stepping-stones. That exceptional therapist, Milton Erickson, always stated that people have within them the information that they need to make the changes they desire.

Part of our challenge as therapists is to help people get in touch with that information, always affirming that the changes they make are their own; we are just facilitators.

The techniques that follow are simply some of the "stepping-stones."

THREE BOXES

We're going to talk about problem solving, today.

Sometimes, if you're going around in circles over something, it really helps to have a good gimmick, just to break the cycle.

introductory comments useful for any problem-solving session

And hypnosis is the ideal state to be in when one is doing this kind of problem solving, because when we take ourselves into hypnosis, we have already taken ourselves one step away from the *immediacy* of the situation, and that in itself is helpful.

N.B. this is a "busy" hyp-nosis with quite a lot of conscious involvement. Your subject may remark that it was "different" from previous experiences. You can explain why it felt that way.

So it's easy to understand why and how so many approaches to problem solving have been devised that use hypnosis as a framework. And, as always in hypnosis, the best of these are always very simple. Certainly the one that I'm going to describe to you today is very simple indeed — almost like a children's kindergarten game.

And that's its main advantage. Because it is so simple, it can be adapted to suit ANY problem; and also because it's so simple you don't have to waste any energy on the *technique* itself; you can direct all your energy towards using it.

simple things are often the best

To make it more interesting for you, let yourself think of some minor problem in your own day-to-day life — some little thing that you just wished you could handle better than you do; nothing earth-shattering — save the big, important ones until you've had a bit more experience — just some little aggravation that you would dearly like to be able to handle more comfortably. Then, as I decribe the technique, you can

brings the subject in as participant rather than just listener (active rather than passive)

apply it to that little situation, and so get a working understanding of it that will be even more helpful to you.

The first thing you do, when using this particular technique, is to allow the problem to separate out into all its component parts. You know, we often think of a problem as being just one thing, but it never is: it's always many things — many facets, many aspects, many points of view; contributions from all kinds of sources; old things and new things, important things and trivial things — and all of these components coalesce to create a situation that we think of as being a problem. So the first thing to do is to let them all separate out again. And soon you will find that they can be separated into three main groups; so in your mind's eye, set up three boxes. And the first box is labelled FROM OTHER PEOPLE.

Into that box, you put *all the parts of the problem, (pause)* that are brought to it by other people. Of course, it's often a temptation for us to think that the whole problem is brought by other people, but we know that's not true. It IS true, however, that usually there are *some* parts of the problem that are brought to it by other people, and these are the parts that are put into the first box.

The second box is labelled FACTS, and into that box you put the things that are simply factual: for instance, if there's a deadline to meet, then the date of the deadline would go into the second box; perhaps also the fact that there IS a deadline. But there may be something about the person who set the deadline that needs to go into the first box. And there may be something about one's *reaction* to the deadline

"...components coalesce to create..." will frequently cause a momentary lapse in *conscious* attention

if you know the person is *not* a visualizer, just say "...so in your mind, set up..."

the subconscious will recognize that you put only the *parts of the problem* into the box, not the people

the "not" is less vital at this level of hypnotic involvement. Use your vocal inflections wisely

that needs to go into the third box, which
of course is the box that we each have for
those parts of the problem that we bring to
it ourselves, in this case, that you bring to
it yourself.

So label the third box with your OWN
NAME, and into that box put all the parts of
the problem that *you* bring to it. Usually these
have to do with our *reaction* to things: fear and
pain and pride and anger, various past experiences, hopes and needs and expectations —
all those things we've talked about before —
as well as the things that are special for you
in this particular situation — they all go into
the third box.

**I have referred to "fear
and pain and . . . anger"
(but not pride) in the
previous session — see
"Homework"**

Now: when you have all the parts of the
problem separated out and they're all in their
appropriate boxes, you take the first box, the
one that's labelled FROM OTHER PEOPLE,
and you *throw it away*. You throw it 'way far
away, as far away as you can possibly throw
it, because — we cannot change other people.
Oh, they may change, of course; but they
will change because of their needs, and their
motivations, and not because of our demands,
nor to meet our specifications. Don't waste
your time and energy, therefore, on those
parts of the problem that are brought to it
by other people. Throw that box away.

**this is why one puts only
the *parts of the problem* into
the box — we do not want
to throw away the people
(they are usually important
people — parents, spouses,
the boss, etc.)**

**no one wants to think of
him/herself as wasting
time and energy**

Similarly, you take the second box, the one
that is labelled FACTS, and you throw that
away too, even farther than the first one,
because — we cannot change facts. The *situation*
may change, yes, but that's different; then you
have a new set of facts. For now, these are
the facts in this situation, they cannot be
changed — throw the box away.

change *may* occur

So: if you take a look at your little aggravation now, you'll find it has a different configuration. For one thing, it's smaller, because you've just thrown two big chunks of it away. And for another, *those parts that are left are the parts that you have some chance of DOING something about!*— and you know yourself, when you have some chance of DOING something, that's a very different feeling than being in a situation in which you feel helpless.

people always relate to this statement

And so we come to the third box.

Here you may wish to separate things out a little further. For instance, there may be some parts of the problem that you bring to it that you truly cannot change. One's age might be such a factor, if it were important in a situation (like retirement); or something that's already happened. Some people put these into the FACTS box, but many put them into the third box because they're so personal.

a personal choice

If there are some such parts of the problem, that you bring to it but that you truly cannot change—you couldn't change them no matter how much you wanted to, or even IF you wanted to—put those into a separate little box and send them winging after the first two boxes because—remember?—you're going to *conserve* your time, your energy AND your resources for much more useful purposes than frittering them away on things you cannot change.

puts their minds at ease because they may not want to change it anyway but may find that hard to admit

Secondly—and this is very important—there may be some parts of the problem that you bring to it, that for some reason, at this time, *you don't want to change!* It doesn't even matter what the reasons are, or how other people might label them. Some people do label things; they might label something as selfish or trivial, for instance; but these are just labels that belong *to other people.* That's the sort of thing that can go into the very, very first box and get thrown away immediately. It matters only that YOU RECOGNIZE THEM. This is the group that get put away in a different place: somewhere *accessible,* where you can take them out and re-assess them whenever it is appropriate for you.

we are not bound by other people's opinions

reassurance that this is O.K.!

And so, finally you're left with a very few parts of the problem, maybe just one or two, that you bring to it, and that you can, AND ARE WILLING, to change.

This is where constructive problem solving always begins. Let yourself find, let yourself perceive some such small, small part of the problem; just some little thing — some minor modification that you might make, for instance, or something that you might begin, or perhaps begin stopping (and usually at this stage, the smaller, the better).

one is not expected to change everything all at once

As you have found it, and made your commit-ment to that first very small change, then you have begun the resolution of your problem; and one day soon — very soon, you'll be surprised — you'll find yourself thinking of this little sit-uation and you'll say to yourself, "Well, for goodness sake, that's not a 'problem,' at all! That's just a situation that I manage very well."

And so you will.   **"You can do it!"**

Usually I offer the Three Boxes approach first; then I often say, "Some people prefer a more metaphorical approach to problem solving — especially if they are using hypnosis as a framework. After all, metaphor is part of the language of the subconscious, the language of hypnosis, as we have talked about before; so it's nice, at times, to use the language that the subconscious understands best and appreciates most. You can just let your conscious *mind enjoy the metaphor — your* subconscious *mind will know just how to adapt it to make it most useful, for you.*"

Then, *I will offer one of the following, depending on my judgment of which is most suitable for that patient at that time.*

ICEBERG METAPHOR

There are many useful problem-solving metaphors. This one is about an iceberg.

You know what an iceberg is, of course — one of those great masses of ice where one-ninth is above the water where you can see it and eight-ninths is underwater where it's hidden.

definition: this usually also applies to any problem

Let us define the "problem," as the iceberg. Then, solving the problem involves melting the iceberg.

new framework

It is very hard to melt an iceberg. It is so huge, and so cold, and the great mass of ice with all that coldness inside, keeps the outside too cold to melt very much anyway.

metaphor for various reasons why a problem may be hard to solve

But it very easy to melt an ice *cube.* So, for purposes of melting this iceberg and therefore solving the problem, look around in your imagination and find some way of knocking a chip of ice from the iceberg — a shoe, perhaps, or a thick stick or a rock — you can find something.

tackle a small part instead

there's always *something* i.e., somewhere, to start

There are many ways to melt that ice cube. You might hold it in your hands, or leave it in the sun, or put it in running water, or stick it on the stove. But what happens when you do melt the ice cube?

many more possibilities

Well, for one thing, as far as the ice cube is concerned, you don't have ice any more, you have water. And water is a very different commodity than ice, with all sorts of different qualities and uses.

when you change one part, that part may change dramatically into something that seems really new

And look at the iceberg. Where you broke off the ice cube, the surface is clean and sparkling, with streaks of beautiful colors—deep, deep greens and blues—because of how tightly the water molecules are packed in the thick ice. And the iceberg is a little bit smaller, and has a slightly different shape and 'though it's hard at this point to appreciate, a tiny bit of the iceberg that was hidden under water is now above the surface where it can be seen.

and all the rest of the problem changes, too: it looks—and *is*—different

more is revealed, often in a small, nonthreatening way

And so, as you continue to break off small ice cubes and melt them, in time you have a very different situation: you have gathered up a wonderful supply of useful water, and that iceberg—at first so huge and terrifying— has an altogether different size and shape, glistening and beautiful with gorgeous colors, something to admire and appreciate.

whole new aspect to the situation and some unexpected fringe benefits

BOULDERS AND BRIDGES

Some people prefer a more metaphorical approach to problem solving in hypnosis.

Imagine yourself trudging up a very steep mountain road. The road is very hot and dusty and precipitous; there are thistles all along the sides, there are huge potholes and where there are no potholes there are huge jagged rocks. You're very tired and there's no relief in sight; and as far as you know, this is the only road to take you where you want to go, and it is very important to you that you go there.

we know that sometimes the road we must take is tough, but the priority is to take it

So there you are, laboriously struggling up this road, tired and miserable — but — you're getting there. Slowly, one foot ahead of the other, step by step, you're getting there.

"take it one step at a time" is a common adage

And then, you go around a bend in the road, and you find that a huge boulder has rolled down from somewhere, completely obstructing the road.

unexpected difficulty

Well, what to do?

Well, you could, if you chose, continue on your journey by pushing the boulder in front of you. It's dreadfully tiring, it takes so much time and energy — uphill, too — but — you could do it. Some people do.

some people apparently do not realize that there may be options and so continue to struggle, stubbornly doing the same things over and over again (see definition of "frustration" p. 25)

However, MAYBE (just maybe) you could take a little of the energy that it would take to push the boulder ahead of you, and instead, push it a little bit to one side — just enough to squee-ee-ze through. Or maybe (just maybe) you could use a little of the time that it would take to push the boulder ahead of you, and instead go off from the main road through the thistles (oh, they're very prickly, but it's just for a few yards), go along beside the road a little way and then cut back up to the main road again.

there *are* options if we can take a different perspective; they may also be difficult, but can eventually clear the way AND it *is* permissible to do this

Either way, you are now on the other side of the boulder! You can continue on your journey AND you can still come back and deal with the boulder in a different way, some time in the future, if you wish to do that.

you have not "burned your bridges" — and can tackle the obstacle at a later time

So let's pretend that you did something like that. You are now on the other side of the boulder, continuing your journey and —

ohhh—the road is worse; it's steeper, it's
hotter, dustier, the potholes are deeper, rocks
are more jagged, even the thistles are higher
and there's STILL no relief in sight—but—
you're gettng there! Footstep after plodding
footstep, you're getting there.

**the new tactic may not
be much fun, either**

Until—you go around another bend in the
road and you find that there's been an earth-
quake or something and a bridge, spanning a
chasm, has fallen away. You can see the rest
of the road continuing on the other side.

**most problems have more
than one stumbling block**

So—what to do?

Well you could, if you chose, continue on your
journey by climbing all the way down the side of
that canyon, across the floor of it, and painfully
pulling yourself up the other side again. It's a
terrible journey—but—some people do that.

metaphor for depression

However, maybe (just maybe) you could use
all your creative imagination and find some
way to throw a temporary bridge across that
chasm. Maybe you could chop down a tree
so that the branches fell on to the other side;
or find some long grasses and make some sort
of rope; or even use a rainbow as a bridge—
SOME way to throw a temporary bridge
across the gap. You only have to get across
once. Then you can continue on your journey,
and you could always come back and explore
that canyon, if it is ever important for you
to do that.

**"You have *within you*, the
knowledge that you
need . . ." (Erickson)**

**and you may want to find
out more about that
obstacle also, at a later
date (perhaps in therapy)**

So perhaps sometime, if you feel you really are
obstructed in some endeavor, you could ask
your subconscious to think of it in terms of
boulders, or bridges, because maybe (just
maybe) there's another way around.

**how to apply this in
self-hypnosis**

OTHER APPROACHES TO PROBLEM SOLVING

As I have said before, there are as many approaches to problem solving as there are people approaching, several times over.

For instance, another approach is to suggest that the person separate the problem into categories or chapters, e.g., a problem having to do with school may have a chapter on teachers/professors, or chapters on the situation at home, on the easy subjects, the difficult subjects, "examinationitis," transportation, the financial dilemma, etc. This is just another variation of the Three Boxes.

Another possibility is that the chapters could be stages in one's life: finding the *patterns* of the various problems in each stage is a fascinating exercise. You could explore that yourself, sometime!

The Leaves on a Pond approach is also easily adaptable to problem solving (see the chapter on Daydreams for Discovery).

If your imagination is temporarily at a standstill, ask your subject to devise some imaginative technique. Often he or she will come up with something far more creative and *à propos* than we can offer.

PROBLEMS IN THE WORKPLACE

Often, clients will come in with their minds focused on problems in the workplace. Such problems may (in their opinion) be affecting their family relationships or social life, and/or adding such stress to their already overburdened selves that it is beginning to interfere with their health—they can't sleep, can't concentrate, have trouble making decisions, get headaches, find their blood pressure rising, etc.

The following are the outlines for five workshops that I have given. They are copyrighted,* but can certainly be used as guidelines for approaching the subjects with your clients. Each of the five is organized into the questions that the client might be asking him/herself, some suggestions for techniques that you as the therapist might use and adapt—or at least help you get started!—and some comment about the outline and its possible application.

These are not scripts, but only suggestions to spur *your* creative self.

1. Creative Decision-Making

Questions

1. What is getting in the way of more creative decision-making?
2. Why am I/we stuck in the old, dull ways?

---

* © 1991 by Marlene E. Hunter, M.D., and SeaWalk Consulting Ltd.

3. Am I anxious about something? my talent? my job? my self-image?
4. How do I break down these barriers, once I have identified them?

Some Techniques

- We are frequently imprisoned by our old patterns; ways to break open the prison gates
- Problem-solving techniques for roadblocks
- What is your definition of a problem? How definitions predicate the outcome
- "Lateral thinking" — Edouard De Bono (1971, 1976) and his contribution
- "Brainstorming" — for one person
  — for a group
  (Brainstorming is the art of letting the imagination run wild, and then harvesting the wild flowers)
- Challenge your subconscious: — use of metaphor
  — as a child would see it
  — if you were the boss next year. . .
  (thanking yourself for the decision)
  — a walk into the future
  — imaging the result
  — finding out what you chose
- Be outrageous! — using a flower in the decision
  — using a tricycle in the decision
  — using a space ship in the decision
- Doodling and its messages
- Personal suggestion box

Comment: The feeling that one cannot make a good decision is one of the most frequent complaints from people under this sort of stress (and other types of stress, too). Giving them some options that will prod *their* imaginations is a practical thing to do. You can adapt these to hypnotic or posthypnotic suggestions with very little effort.

2. Strengthening Inner Resources

Questions:

1. Do I *have* any Inner Resources?
2. Where and what are they?
3. Why have I not been able to use them?

Some Techniques:

- The "Hunter Quartet": Identifying Strengths
    Acknowledging Frailties
    Reviewing Past Successes
    Clarifying "Shoulds"
- Ego-Strengthening
    affirmations
    language
    self-talk
- Understanding the Stress Response (and then utilizing it!)
- Metaphor — your Pool of Resources
    contributions from your successes
    contributions from your worst scenarios
      "If only I'd known then. . . . "
      "The best thing that ever happened. . .!!"
        — Train Metaphor (Rossi: "How can I utilize something
    that I do well, to help me to do something else, better?")
- Meditation/Imagery/Self-hypnosis techniques
- Sharing and receiving strengths with/from others
- "YOU KNOW MORE THAN YOU KNOW THAT YOU
  KNOW" — Milton Erickson

Comment: This seminar or workshop is directed to helping people reappraise their own resources in order to feel more self-confident, able to handle whatever comes their way.

3. Dealing With Self-Identity in a Large Corporation

Questions:

1. Do I *have* any self-identity in this corporation?
2. Am I just a litle cog in the wheel?
3. Could "just anybody" do my job, and do it just as well as I? Better than I?
4. What if I goof up? (i.e., make a significant blunder)

Some Techniques:

- Identity can get lost in a big corporation
    — too insignificant a person; too insignificant a role

- Does anybody know I'm here?
    - how did you get the job in the first place?
- Can I really do this job?
    - assessing qualifications, experience, education
    - worse if one needs the job
    - afraid to make waves
- "There's nothing wrong with Duddy Kravitz!" (a different way of thinking about things)
- Daily ego-strengthening
    - self-talk and how to use it
- The case of the overpowering superior:
    - of whom does he/she remind you?
    - no access to the hierarchy
- What if I goof up?
    - dealing with clients
    - will I do it right?
    - what if I can't answer the questions?
- Making one's own niche
    - highest quality of which one is capable
    - ask for regular evaluations, if possible
    - suggestion box
    - chances for advancement
- A linchpin, not a cog!

Comment: This workshop is to help people to engage in self-evaluation in a supportive milieu. Self-identity, or the absence thereof, creates more stress than most other aspects of the workplace.

4. Coping With Irate Clients

Questions:

1. How do I "keep my cool"?
2. What if I say or do the wrong thing and make the situation worse?
3. Will my boss think that it was all my fault?
4. What if *I* believe it was all my fault?

Some Techniques:

- Remember, the CLIENT is irate, not you!

- Fear that you may have done something wrong:
  - starts the stress response going
  - what the stress response is and how to reverse and/or utilize it
- You are the one on the firing line
  - different from being responsible for the situation happening
  - how to avoid being defensive
  - how to avoid the *"It's not fair!"* reaction
- Assertiveness vs aggressiveness
  - role-playing submissive/assertive/aggressive
- Client interaction:
  - *clarify* the complaint
  - respectfully rephrase if appropriate
  - allowing clients to express themselves fully
  - responding that you appreciate their distress (not the same as agreeing with the complaint)
  - avoid offering the moon
  - assure that the matter will be investigated if you cannot deal with the whole issue yourself
  - ascertain exactly what the client wants
- Understanding the roots of anger
- The vital importance of language
- Transference and countertransference issues

Comment: This workshop deals with the very practical "how-to" issues of client interaction.

5. Discovering the Inner Partnership:
The Interaction of Moods and Performance

Questions:

1. Do my moods influence my performance? How?
2. Can I utilize these facts to my advantage? How?
3. What IS the "Inner Partnership"?
4. How can I compensate for unfavourable moods?

Some Techniques:

- Understanding ego-states
  - what they are
  - how they manifest in everyday life

- Stress is a positive force
  - understanding the stress response
  - utilizing the positive stress
- Hormonal influences
  - stress, PMS, thyroid function, etc.
- State-dependent learning:
  - how what we learned before, influences behavior now (based on Rossi's work)
- Which actor is on tonight?
  - Philosopher/psychologist/employer/fixer-upper/mystic — who is interacting to produce the performance you need for this situation?
  - assets from various roles: the wide-eyed child, the serious student, the parent, the businessman/woman, the professor, etc.

Comment: This workshop promotes understanding of the various aspects of one's life and personality, past experience and present milieu, and how these factors interact in order to present the most favorable performance in any situation. It is directed to the "together" person who has some understanding of his/her own ego states.

Obviously, all of these outlines can be used for ego-strengthening as well as for offering opportunities for a new problem-solving approach. I have included them here to stimulate and provoke your own creativity.

6

Reframing

"Reframing" simply refers to organizing a new context for the situation.

It is a concept that is used extensively in NeuroLinguistic Programming (NLP); however, here I am using it in a simpler connotation.

Most people will understand the concept if you ask them whether they have ever taken an old familiar picture, that they have looked at thousands of times, out of its old frame and replaced that frame with a new one, perhaps a different color, size, or shape, or a new matting around the picture.

Anyone who has ever done this will immediately agree that the picture, *which has not changed,* looks entirely different in its new frame. If people have never done that, invite them to do so before their next visit and they will return amazed by what they saw with their own eyes, and in a very willing "frame of mind" to apply that new knowledge to their own situation.

The reframing vocabulary lends itself wonderfully to this process, as you will see for yourself.

You may find it interesting to read some of the early work in the field of NLP/Reframing. In particular, the books and articles by Bandler and Grinder (1979, 1982) will set the scene nicely.

For a more up-to-date and sophisticated discourse, the papers by Dr. D. Ebrahim (1988) in the Swedish Journal of Clinical and Experimental Hypnosis offer thought-provoking concepts to those of an inquiring mind regarding the neurological rationale behind NeuroLinguistic Programming.

REWRITE THE SCRIPT

(The patient is NOT in hypnosis when this script begins)

Last week, when you were in hypnosis, you
were remembering a very painful old experience.

(You may wish to make some specific reference to that experience. I usually just leave it with the general statement, not knowing what else the subconscious might have had on its mind.)

And we agreed that this week we would explore some ways to bring some healing to that old experience.

So often, we think to ourselves, "If only I had known then, what I know now, I would have done it differently." Well, of course we would have! The point is, we did NOT know that, what we know now, and we did *the very best we could with the information that we had!* I am sure that YOU did the very best that YOU could do, at that time, with the information that you had.

validating previous decisions

We also have a great tendency to think that if we had done something ELSE, everything would have been better. *But we have no way of knowing that.* The ONLY thing we can know, is that if we had done something different, the following events would have been different.

We have no way of knowing whether they would have been better, or worse, or neither— only that they would have been different.

obviating guilt/blame

Now that you know more, you can see alternatives that, in retrospect, seem better. And luckily for us, we have a great tool for utilizing this new knowledge. We can, in hypnosis, go back and reexperience it THE WAY YOU WISH IT HAD BEEN. Of course, your conscious mind knows full well what we are doing, but nevertheless, the subconscious mind can use the hypnotic experience to help heal the old pain.

new information now available

reason for using hypnosis

"healing the old pain" is a comforting phrase

Just get yourself comfortably settled, then,
and watch my thumb as it comes slowly down
to touch your forehead, letting your eyes close
gently, feeling that little flickering in your
eyelids and then taking yourself into hypnosis
in your own way to whatever level is just right
for you to achieve what you are going to
achieve today. That's right.

"achieve what you are going to achieve" — hypnotic suggestion for success

And when you know that you have reached
that right level, just let me know by taking
a deep breath.

(Stay comfortably silent, allowing the patient to reach his or her own best level)

(When the ideomotor signal is given) Good. You
are very safe now, here in hypnosis in my office,
at the level of hypnosis that is just right for you
at this time.

Now when you feel my thumb on your forehead
again, let your subconscious mind go backwards
in time, to the time when that old painful experience began. Yes, that's right. And, protected
as you are, safe as you are here in my office,
let your subconscious mind review that old
experience. That's right. Just let the tears flow.
Let them wash away some of that old pain.
Is it alright if I wipe the tears for you? Fine.
I'll take care of that, you just let them flow.

identifying a painful experience is possible when one is protected

(Never touch without permission)

When your inner mind has finished reviewing
that experience, let me know. *(Patient nods)* Good.

Now. Let your subconscious mind go back
again to that time, and this time experience
it THE WAY YOU WISH IT HAD BEEN,
bringing to that new interpretation all the
information, understanding, knowledge, and

utilizing the new information and integrating it

experience that you have gained since that occasion, all that life has taught you since then. That's right, bring all that new learning and awareness as you reframe that old experience now into this new scenario. Yes, that's right. You know exactly how to do that. Good.

re-view, re-frame scenario — all complement the same concept: re-view — "see again"

And when you have finished that reframing, again let your subconscious mind review that new interpretation, seeing it as if for the first time. Yes, that's very good.

referring to previous suggestion

As you are doing that, be aware within your own self of the healing that has occurred and is occurring. FEEL that healing. Yes, be soothed and eased by that healing.

"feel the healing" — onomatopoetic

(*Speaking very softly now*) That's right. Feel the healing. Yes.

Stay there a little longer — as long as you wish in hypnotic time, while I watch the clock time for you. Yes. Let that healing ease away all the old painful memory, so that you now have just the distant memory, perceived in this new way, without the pain.

acknowledge the *fact* of the old experience, and the *perceptual* change

BODY LANGUAGE

This term can mean the posture of the body, and the meaning that conveys, and the use of idiomatic language such as, "You make me sick," "Keep a stiff upper lip," "Stand on your own two feet," etc. As we listen carefully to what our patients are saying, and *how they are saying it,* we will be able to glean a great deal of information from their body language.

The terminology can be used both ways — by them as they describe their situation to us, or by us as we rephrase their situation to them. For example, the patient who is scratching him/herself to pieces could be asked gently (as I have done with one memorable patient), "What is getting under your skin so badly that you are using this way to describe it?" Or the patient who comes in saying,

"My stomach's in a knot all the time"—and, of course, is having gastrointestinal symptoms.

English abounds in such phrases—and I'm sure other languages do, too. We can use that language capacity to clarify symptomatology. Many times, patients will not recognize the double meaning until it is pointed out to them—and then there is immediate recognition.

You can also obtain considerable insight by observing posture, tension, how or whether the arms are folded over the body protectively, and many other clues. Jiggling or repetitive movements also offer silent commentary as to the patient's emotional discomfort.

Then we can turn around and utilize all this information in the way we phrase our hypnotic suggestions.

Case History

Mrs. A.J., 59 years of age, was referred because of bruxism. She told me that she had been grinding her teeth for years, ever since she was a teenager, and her dentist despaired of ever being able to repair the damage. Mouth guards made her gag. She certainly did not want to have her whole dentition extracted, but that might be what she would be facing not too far down the line.

She denied knowing any instigating cause for the grinding and said that her life was happy ". . . as much as any reasonable person could expect." She had been married 22 years, has a son and daughter, both in their teens, and she was in good health. She said she slept well. She worked part-time as an accountant, which suited her perfectly as it gave her time for home and family, but also brought in a little extra cash and kept her in contact with the business world.

After the usual first two sessions, which she professed to have enjoyed, she was restless at the third session. I had already told her that, at this session, we would begin to pay more attention to those issues of personal concern to her.

This is a tip-off, so I asked MY subconscious for inspiration. What I (or my subconscious) came up with was, "Ask your subconscious mind, now, to take you back to some situation that had gone on for a long time, had really begun to grind you down. Ask for some information about that, something that would help you to understand something else about yourself that you need to know."

She began to cry. "What is happening?" I asked, softly. She was in high school, she said. She was trying her best, but it never seemed good enough. To whom? "To my father. He just kept at me all the time, all the time, all the time. I began to hate school, even though I was good at it."

I asked if it would be alright, now, for her conscious mind to remember more, and she nodded, yes.

After she came out of her hypnosis, we talked about the session. Never did SHE refer to "grinding" or "being ground down" and I did not mention it again. After several more sessions, she used the hypnotic framework to tell her father (in absentia) how his constant criticism had made her feel. After she came out of hypnosis, she commented, "I guess I really mouthed off at him, didn't I?"

POSITIVE MODE/WORDS AND MEANINGS

It is essential to explain to the person who wishes to make changes with the help of hypnosis how to phrase suggestions in such a way that the subconscious will perceive the real message very clearly.

It is equally important to explain that we are giving these messages to our subconscious minds all the time, without even realizing it!

Always phrase suggestions in the positive mode. The subconscious mind tends to ignore the word "not" and all its variants. To give an immediate example of this, ask the person: "Please DO NOT think of a pink elephant." A few moments later, comment, "You're not thinking of a pink elephant, right?" Of course, the person will be thinking of a pink elephant, and the point is made.

You can explain that words and logic belong to the language of the conscious, computing mind. Imagery, metaphor, symbolism, parable — those belong to the language of the subconscious mind; and it is very difficult to have a negative image, because the mind creates the very image that the words are telling it to "not have."

Rather than say, "I'm not going to worry," say, "I feel calm." You can give several explicit examples, using the person's own concerns so that he/she can focus clearly on how applicable these comments are.

There are also some very sabotaging words, and people need to be aware of these, also.

The most sabotaging word in the English language, in my opinion, is the word "TRY"; every time we use this word, there is always the implicit possibility of failure. Somewhere, at the back of the mind, is the little voice that says, "You might not make it." There are many things one can do instead of "try": one can search, learn, discover, explore, find out more about — and all of these have a more positive connotation than "try." Best of all, just *do* it. I strongly urge people to listen to themselves, and every time they hear themselves using the word "try," go through the routine of rephrasing the sentence using one of the other words. The whole feeling of the sentence is changed. Explore this for yourself!

"Shoulds" are discussed in another session (p. 146).

It is just as important to offer explicit suggestions for reframing the person's "problem." "I always mess everything up" becomes "I've learned some valuable lessons." "I'll never get well" changes to "It is discouraging to be ill for a long time; I'm looking forward to feeling better." With teenagers, this can take the form of a challenge game — let's see who can come up with the best alternative first, or the most alternatives, or the "farthest out" alternative, etc.

These are good challenges for the therapist, too — using ingenuity and humor to bring a new perspective to an old, demoralizing situation.

CREATING A "WIB"

(One of the major problems for anxious people is the overwhelming tendency to think "But what if. . .?" This is followed with terrifying images of worst-case scenarios. The following is a useful little gimmick to help many patients get past that roadblock.)

We've talked about the difficulty you have when the scary "What IF . . ." thoughts flood over you. So it's a good idea to organize, for yourself, a way to immediately neutralize those thoughts.

recognizing the situation and offering some way to change it

In your own imagination, create a "WIB." Yes, a "WIB." A "WIB" is a "What-If-Box" and there are some very important attributes for a successful "WIB."

(this can be said with amusement in the voice at first, then become more serious again)

First it must be a "WIB" that exactly suits YOU. "WIBs" are very, *very* personal. It must be just the right size and shape and made of exactly the right materials.

There must be a *one-way* opening into the "WIB."

so the deposits cannot come back out again; this deflects another "What If. . .?"

Every good "WIB" is *absolutely, completely, totally safe.* So take a little time, now, to construct your own personal "WIB" and do whatever you need to do to ensure that complete security. I'll just be quiet, while you do that, and you can nod your head or take a deep breath to let me

personal involvement; this is *his or her* "WIB," not mine or yours.

know when you have finished your "WIB"
to meet all your important criteria.

*(Keep silent until the patient gives you the signal.
If it seems to be taking a very long time, you can
say, softly, "That's right, you are taking care of all
the important details and your 'WIB' is nearly
finished.")*

**"You are doing all the
right things"—the patient
may be fretting over
possible mistakes**

Good. You're doing a wonderful job of
creating your "WIB."

reinforcement

Now, this is how the "WIB" works.

down to the practicalities!

EVERY time you hear yourself saying—aloud
or silently—"What if. . .?" or feel any of those
emotions that are part of "What ifs," or
become aware that your body is responding
to the "What if?" feelings with any of those
anxiety symptoms you know so well, then you
IMMEDIATELY send ALL those thoughts,
words, emotions, and sensations *right into the
"WIB"*—PChooo!!

Because you know that your "WIB" is
completely secure and all of those thoughts
and feelings will be perfectly safe in there for
as long as is necessary. And with those taken
care of, you can get on with other things.

the desired result

And that brings us to the last important point
about "WIBs." It's very strange, and who
knows how it happens, but everything that is
consigned to a "WIB" stays there until the *time
for the possible eventuality has passed!* And THEN—
it spontaneously evaporates!

**removing the remaining
"What if?"**

That means that there is always room in your
"WIB," any time you need to deposit another
"What if. . .?" in it.

trance logic

Give yourself an opportunity to practice using your "WIB," while you are still here in your hypnosis. Let yourself think of some typical situation which would cause a "What if?" for you; then, as soon as you have recognized that — Ppchooo! Into the "WIB" it goes!

beginning the desensitization process

Now feel that freedom in yourself, when you have done that! You KNOW that your "What If?" is safe and sound, and will stay securely in the "WIB" as long as it needs to.

That's right. That's how it works.

reassurance

When you are doing your own hypnosis at home, practice using your "WIB," just as you have done here. Then, when you need it, you will know exactly how to do it.

practice brings results

THE CHILD WITHIN

The concept of the Inner Child has been popularized by John Bradshaw in books, workshops, and TV shows. His premise is that family dysfunction so affects the child that he or she carries the pain throughout life, expressing it in ways that can metaphorically be attributed to the child's response. Using some form of hypnotic approach, albeit often informally, one makes contact with that Inner Child and comforts and reassures him/her, thus doing a kind of self-reparenting.

It is a slightly different concept from feeling childish or (better) childlike at times, and also very different from the fully dissociated child alters found in Multiple Personality Disorder (Dissociative Identity Disorder) patients — the latter, of course, quite outside the scope of this book.

The Child Within is a useful concept but may need to be explained for what it is — a metaphor for understanding the self when we behave or respond in ways that seem inappropriate or overdone.

COMFORTING THE CHILD WITHIN

You have learned a great deal in the past few weeks, about why things have been happening

the way they have, and about new ways of   **reframing suggestion**
perceiving, and therefore of being able to
change those old responses.

But there is one part of you, deep within,
that we must give some time and attention
to, today. I am talking about the child within.

We all have our childhood selves deep within
us. Indeed, those are the selves who sent us on
our way, who first perceived and discovered   **there is nothing "odd"**
how to interpret the world. Our perceptions,   **about the premise**
our discoveries and interpretations change as
we grow into adulthood, but that child within
in still there, wondering and exploring and
responding.

Today, then, we are going to go back to visit
with that Child Within YOU, the child who
first encountered these experiences that are
concerning you.

Settle yourself more comfortably and   **opportunity for deeper**
take yourself to whatever level of hypnosis   **hypnosis for this**
is just right for you at this time. That's right.   **experience**

And turn your attention to a typical
occasion when you . . .*(describe the situation
with which the patient is concerned)*. Yes, good.

And let yourself begin to really experience that
situation, the way you have been experiencing
it. Be particularly aware of the FEELINGS   **creating an affect bridge**
that come with that experience, the feelings
that may almost overwhelm you at times.

Now, when you feel my thumb on your   **(my usual technique)**
forehead, let your subconscious mind go
backwards in time, backwards in time to the
time when you *first felt those FEELINGS.*   **completing the bridge**

That's right, backwards in time to the time when you first felt those feelings. Find yourself there, experiencing those feelings. I think you will find a little child there, a little child who feels confused, frightened, and perhaps in pain and maybe with all kinds of other feelings, too — a little child who is doing his *(her)* very BEST to understand and to do the right things, but is so confused and unhappy — ah, yes, you have found that small child, that's right — that little child who needs you so much because, you see, you are the ONLY ONE who *really* knows what that small child is feeling, the only one who can really understand and, therefore, the only one whom that child can REALLY trust.

"find yourself. . .(as) a little child there"

reaffirming the child

(watch carefully for subtle signs)

no one else knows your feelings

Comfort that little child. Hold him *(her)*, soothe and comfort him. Tell him that he's a GOOD BOY, and that you KNOW that he's a good boy, and that he has *always* done his very best, the very best that he could do. And let him know how much you respect him for that, for always doing his very best, as you KNOW that he has done.

ego-strengthening of child will, of course, strengthen the adult

And somehow — I don't know how you're going to do this, but I know that you can — find the way to explain to him whatever it is that he needs to understand, so that he can feel better. Explain to him that although he is very confused and unhappy right now, you KNOW that *he is going to be alright!* And you are the ONLY one who can tell him that and whom he can truly believe. That's right. Comfort, soothe, and reassure that child.

subjects do find their own ways of communicating with themselves

feelings of trust can be very difficult, depending on the depth of childhood trauma — and remember, the reality of the child is different from the reality of the adult

And let him know, also, that you will be spending more time with him after this, to get to know him better. You have so much to give to him. And HE HAS SO MUCH TO GIVE

implying future exploration

TO YOU, TOO—he has many gifts for you:
the creativity and joy of childhood, the spirit
of exploration and wonderment. You have
gifts for each other.

**opportunity to recapture
some of one's youthful
enthusiasm**

So let him know that you will be coming back
to visit with him. And that, if he ever needs to
visit with you, he can reach you by just knocking on the door of the subconscious and asking
you to come. What YOU will notice, perhaps,
is that you suddenly feel as if you would like to
go into hypnosis for a little while—perhaps to
visit with your younger self. In that way you
will hear him when he calls you.

**metaphor for allowing
oneself to recognize
feelings of insecurity**

So say goodbye to him for now, reassuring
him again and letting him know that you will
be visiting often. That's right. And then when
you have said goodbye, stay in hypnosis, but
bring yourself back to this present time *(say
the date)* in my office.

THANK THE PROTECTOR

*(The patient is in hypnosis, and you have been
addressing some behavior pattern or response or habit
which he/she wishes to change, but somehow seems
unable to do so.)*

Remember that all patterns begin for a purpose;
we may wonder, at this stage of our lives, what
on earth that purpose was, because it may remain
a mystery to us—but we can be assured that it
must have seemed very important to the subconscious at the time, because it has been
doing its best to protect it for us, ever since.

**validating the original
behavior**

But we all tend, at times, to get trapped by
our old patterns, too.

**this happens to all of us,
not just you**

You are in that situation now. You are stuck in this pattern, which you are sure you want to change.

Then you must give this message strongly to your subconscious mind, while *at the same time* recognizing and respecting that that deep inner part of you has been doing what it thought it needed to do. So say to your own deep inner self, in your own words, something like this: "Thank you for your good intentions. I realize that you have been just doing what you thought was best, what you believed needed to be done. *Why* you believed that, is somewhat confused for me, something of a mystery, but I do understand that that was your reasoning.

> the matter of *respect* is extremely important because it obviates the tendency to guilt/blame

"However, those old reasons, whatever they were, belong to the past. I now need a new pattern for the present and the future. Please help me formulate such a new pattern now, and put the old reasons respectfully away. Their task is now finished."

> providing the subconscious with good reason to change

> "task is finished" implies job well done

Repeat this information to yourself many times in the next few days and weeks. Your subconscious mind must be completely reassured that you DO need new responses, before it will let the old ones, that it has been protecting *with the best of intentions* for so long, be replaced.

Thank your Inner Protector. It has always done, and will continue to do, the very best that it believes it must do, for you.

> ego-strengthening

TRAIN METAPHOR

Often when we are faced with a course of action that seems unfamiliar to us, we think

that because we have never been in that
situation before, we know nothing about it.

reassurance that this is a common experience

In those circumstances, it may be useful to
think of the situation as similar to one in which
a person is about to take a journey on a train,
but is nervous because he or she has never
taken a train journey before, and thinks that
she/he knows nothing about it.

Let us call this person, "Mrs. Smith."

Now, Mrs. Smith may never have been on a
train before, but she *has* been on a bus. Furthermore, she has travelled on a bus to another
city, so she knows how to read a timetable and
find out about departure and arrival times
(after all, she had to let the people that she
was visiting in the other city, know when she
was arriving).

preparing for the train journey

Having done that, she also knows how to go
to the depot and buy a ticket; she even knows
how to phone ahead to make sure that the bus
will leave on time and find out whether she has
to reserve a seat or just pick up the ticket when
she gets to the station.

When she gets to the station, she knows how
to find the right bay, where the bus is parked.
She has some suitcases, so she knows how to
take them to the place where they will be
checked for the journey, and she even gets a
little ticket because it is quite a long journey
and there are many passengers and therefore
there are many pieces of luggage.

embarking

And when she took the bus trip, she chatted
in a comfortable, friendly way with the people
sitting next to her. At the end of the journey,

passing the time comfortably

she knows how to find the special place
to hand in her little ticket and reclaim her
suitcases, and go through the big bus depot
to where the taxis are, or to meet her friends
who have come to pick her up.

arriving

And Mrs. Smith may never have been on a
train before, but she has travelled by car, so
she knows about watching the scenery go by
and perhaps even following her progress on a
map. She has often eaten in restaurants, so she
knows how to go into the dining car, to wait to
be seated, consult the menu, and order a meal;
and then how to pay for the meal and leave a tip.

enjoying the new experience

mealtimes

Because she has visited other cities or has
stayed with friends, she knows what it is like
to sleep in a strange bed. And when she was
a little girl, she loved being rocked to sleep!

**regression to childhood
(deepening and anchoring)**

In fact, Mrs. Smith knows almost all there
is to know about travelling on a train except
actually being on a train. It is just that all of
this information has been scattered around in
a variety of different experiences, and needed
to be gathered up and reapplied to the new
circumstances.

**"you have within you, all
the information..."**

For this present situation in which you find yourself, then, ask your subconscious mind to go
gathering all the information it can find that
may in some way relate to it — a little bit of
information from that past experience, more
information from another experience — and
put them all together in a *new package,* one that
is useful and appropriate for this particular time.

reframing

You know far more than you know that you
know. Enjoy discovering the wonderful range
of your own knowledge.

ego-strengthening

7

Research

Achieving relief from pain is one of the most sought-after effects of hypnosis.

There are different types of pain — chronic and acute, for example — and different situations: surgery, childbirth, debilitating diseases, posttraumatic, phantom limb, etc.

Luckily there are also limitless hypnotic approaches for pain relief. This section explores a few of them.

A BIT OF HISTORY

In 1978 I attended the First European Congress of Hypnosis and Hypnotherapy in Psychosomatic Medicine and Psychotherapy in Mälmo, Sweden. At that time I heard Professor Barry Wyke, of London, England, define pain as "Pain is an emotion." The audience shifted posture somewhat — this was an unusual definition, to say the least, and no one was quite sure what to make of it.

He went on to explain his definition. Pain is a response to a stimulus, a response that can be both emotional and physiological. We know that people respond very differently to what is apparently the same physiological stimulus — therefore, the emotional part of the response is what, for most people, constitutes "pain."

His way of presenting "pain" was meant to provoke our attention, and it did. There is no doubt that I remember his words every time a chronic pain sufferer and I launch off on a mutual journey to look for ways and means of relieving pain.

CURRENT CONCEPTS

The gate theory of Melzack and Wall (1965) is probably the most widely accepted theory of pain perception today. It says, in effect, that other perceptions can (if they arrive first) close the "gate" through which pain perception travels to the brain. This explains the relief brought by massage, transcutaneous electrical nerve stimulation, heat or cold, etc.

As this theory (as well as others) of pain has to do with *perception,* and hypnosis has to do with altering perception, we can begin to understand a little more about hypnotic pain relief. We are changing the perception of pain so as to relieve the suffering component.

An excellent book by an Australian author, Leonard Rose (1990), who is a pain management specialist and director of one of Australia's first pain management clinics, provides a valuable section on hypnosis, imagery, and acupuncture.

Up to Date

At present there is a great deal of research into the phenomena of phantom limb pain, much of it by Katz (1992, 1993), a young colleague of Melzack. He has identified that the presence of pre-amputation pain is necessary for the survivor to experience phantom-limb pain; it is as if there were a "memory" of the pain in the phantom limb. This concept has great relevance for survivors of child abuse, who have long spoken of "body memories" of their abuse and have too often been denigrated for their insistance.

Another interesting piece of research by these authors is their paper (1986) on the role of compensation in chronic pain. Many people who are on some sort of compensation for injuries suffered on the job or in a motor vehicle accident are accused of prolonging the pain for financial gain. This study refuted that, using techniques such as the McGill Pain Questionnaire and the Minnesota Multiphasic Personality Inventory, and indicated that compensation patients do not exaggerate their pain or show greater symptoms of neurotic psychopathology than other chronic pain patients.

It seems to me that chronic pain syndromes are dissociative in nature and have much in common with other chronic disorders — fibromyalgia, chronic fatigue syndrome, etc. It is as if one part of the person takes over and *becomes pain.* This offers great opportunity for inventive hypnotic approaches (Hunter, 1989), which I will discuss in more detail later in this book.

One thing we know — the usual medication approaches do NOT work well for patients with chronic pain or with phantom-limb pain — which behooves us to explore alternative approaches with vigor.

8

Hypnotic Techniques for Pain Relief

Today I shall describe some of the basic ways in which we can use hypnosis for the relief of pain.

They fall into a number of main categories, and then the techniques are modified by the person to suit him or her individually.

The first category is really hypnosis itself, or meditation or yoga or any other altered state of consciousness, because in hypnosis (or other altered states) the muscles in the body tend to release their tension. We sometimes refer to that as being "relaxed," but it is a very special form of relaxation; the mind may be very active or it may be daydreaming, that is quite variable, but the muscles "relax," they release their tension.

Tight muscles tend to be more uncomfortable than relaxed muscles, therefore relaxing those muscles will bring relief. You can test this yourself by clenching your fist tightly, then releasing it. All pain (no matter what the origin of the pain) has some muscle-tension component because the natural tendency of the body in pain is to splint, to hold the painful part still or hold it tight. That is helpful, but at the same time it contributes to one kind of pain. With

pain *relief* has more comfortable possibilities than pain *control,* which implies that the pain will be there but the person is *controlling* it

describing the rationale

some pain there is more of the tension
component and with other pain it is less,
but it is always there.

Think, for instance, of a man going in to the
Emergency Room with a broken arm. He holds
the arm tightly to himself, it is very painful, he
doesn't dare move it. A little while later, when
the plaster cast is on, the arm has quickly
become more comfortable. Why? Because now
the *cast* is holding the arm still, and so the
muscles can relax.

familiar examples to which everyone can relate

So releasing muscle tension relieves that part
of the pain that is due to muscle tension, and
because all pain does have that component to
some degree, there is always something that
one can do to relieve that part of the pain. And
it is always very reassuring to know that there
is something one can do to bring *some* relief.

being able to *do* something is always better than feeling helpless

The second group has to do with dissociation
techniques: ways to put a barrier or some distance between you and the pain. People tend
to become very imaginative about these. Some
people, for instance, take the pain and put it
on a shelf somewhere or leave the painful part
of the body in bed or in a comfortable chair
while they get up and go about their tasks.

invitation to be one of those imaginative people

Some people, in their imaginations, put some
sort of a buffer — styrofoam, a vacuum, glass —
between themselves and the pain. When a person
devises some such sort of barrier or some
distance, it is almost as if one were looking
at the pain from the outside and indeed that is
what some people seem to be doing. When one
is looking at pain from the outside or from a
distance, it is much less a part of you and
therefore it intrudes less on your awareness.

trance logic

The third major group consists of substitution possibilities and there are at least three ways to substitute. First, one can substitute a different feeling for the pain, such as numbness or warmth or tingling or pressure (all of which are more comfortable than pain); this is rather an easy translation to make. Secondly, it is sometimes useful to substitute a different place in the body to experience the pain. For instance, if the pain is deep within you somewhere, you might want to bring it out to the surface where you could massage it. If you have a headache and you have a term paper to finish, put the pain in some other part of the body where it bothers you less and then you can get to work.

you can fill in any specific situations that apply to your patient

Thirdly, one can substitute a different time to experience the pain. This is a technique that people often do spontaneously. Athletes who are injured in a competition often don't even know they are injured until the competition is over; a mother will ignore her own pain and injuries until she knows her child is safe. These are fairly common, spontaneous episodes of substituting a different time to appreciate pain. If we can do something spontaneously, we can learn to do it on purpose.

frequent use of the word "can" reassures the subject that it is possible

familiar examples, again, to which people easily relate

You may even have some similar experience of saying, "I don't have time for this headache right now!" — and a short while later, you realize the headache has gone.

The fourth major group of techniques consists of ways to change the image of the pain (and by now you are realizing that these techniques all overlap to a great degree).

Pain does have an image. It may have a size, a shape, an edge, a color, a consistency, a density, a mood, a temperature, a sound — all of these are ways to describe the image of a pain: a throbbing headache; a red, hot, angry joint.

these descriptions will evoke the person's own imagery

One must first decipher what the image of one's pain is. Then, one considers how the image must change to become comfortable. Perhaps the red must change to pearly-pink, the heat subsiding to cool, and anger easing away to a more serene feeling. And when we change the image, an amazing thing happens: the pain changes, too, and subsides to a more comfortable awareness.

again, some familiar examples

note "awareness": we are talking about *analgesia*, not anesthesia

Usually, the most workable way to accomplish this is to change one factor at a time — first change the color, then the temperature, then the mood. What happens as we accomplish those changes in our imaginations is fascinating and quite remarkable.

The fifth main group consists of a variety of specialized techniques such as the extremely simple and useful breathing technique — simply drawing in comfortable feelings from the most comfortable part of your body as you breathe in, and sending them where they are needed as you breathe out.

Children like to work the rheostat — they can turn it up or they can turn it down — or they enjoy imagining there is a little black box in their heads that has "pain switches" to various parts of the body, which they can then simply switch off! (And sometimes, because we are all children at heart, these things do work with grown-ups, too.)

turning the pain *up* would be met with incredulity in the alert state but may be accepted in the hypnotic; however, they are happy to turn it down again, thus learning the valuable lesson that they *can* change it

So you have heard me describe a variety
of ways in which we can use the framework
of hypnosis to relieve the suffering of pain.
Consider these in your own time, your own
way, and sense which of them may be most
useful for you. Then you can modify them
to suit your own special needs.

we are relieving the *suffering*

BREATHING

We often use breathing patterns to help us
in hypnosis, in various ways.

For instance, you can use your breathing,
as I'll describe in a minute, to help transfer
comfortable feelings from your most
comfortable part of the body (your own
storehouse of comfortable feelings) to some
other part that needs a little extra; and you
can do that by *borrowing the comfortable feelings
as you breathe in,* sort of ABSORBING them
in, and then *sending them where they're needed
as you breathe out.*

**simple statement, presume
the positive**

Just do that now: borrow the comfortable
feelings as you breathe in *(breathe in deeply
and obviously)* and SEND THEM WHERE
THEY'RE NEEDED AS YOU BREATHE
OUT *(breathing out very noticeably with a soft
blowing sound).* That's right. *Breathe comfortable
feelings in as you breathe in (demonstrating as before)*
and send them RIGHT THROUGH YOUR
BODY WHERE THEY ARE NEEDED as
you breathe out.

**watch the subject's
breathing pattern and
coincide — (s)he will soon
follow yours**

Good. And again — borrowing in as you
breathe in — that's right! Good! And sending
those most comfortable feelings right through
your body as you breathe out. That's excellent.

Just keep on with that in your own rhythm, for a little longer — breathing in comfortable feelings, then sending them through your body, breathing away discomfort and tension at the same time.

"own rhythm" turns the experience completely back to the subject

This is a very easy little technique to learn, and to practice, and to do — and you don't have to be in hypnosis to do that, although you may choose to be. But some people like to practice when they're waiting for a bus, or caught in a traffic jam, or waiting in a doctor's office, or watching TV, or visiting friends — wherever it might be, just find your most comfortable place, borrow those most comfortable feelings in as you breathe in, and send them where they're needed as you breathe out.

"very easy," therefore everyone can do it

And you will find that you can become very, very good at that.

presumes success

And who knows — maybe some day, that little technique might be very useful for you, and then you'll have it, all ready to adapt to your special needs, at that particular time.

you are prepared

OTHER TECHNIQUES

1. Specific imagery

These would include imagery of the blood vessels returning to their normal diameters (smaller if they are dilated, or larger if they are constricted and/or in spasm) to relieve migraine headache, or muscle fibers, thus releasing spasm, becoming soft and pliable, resting harmoniously beside their fellow fibers.

2. Post-hypnotic suggestion

A "cue" word or phrase that has been established while the patient is in hypnosis can be extremely useful in maintaining or reestablishing relief during a busy day or when it is inappropriate to take time out for a more formal hypnosis. It is important that the patient decide on the word, rather than the therapist; many patients prefer to keep the word private (ESPECIALLY CHILDREN!). If pressed to tell what the word is, many people would feel foolish in choosing something very personal or somewhat fanciful — yet such a word might bring an emotional quality that would add immeasurably to its efficacy.

Rossi has referred frequently to the importance of the emotional component for connecting with the subconscious (Rossi, 1986; Rossi & Cheek, 1988).

3. Glove Anesthesia

Using hypnotic suggestion, the hand (and perhaps wrist and forearm) becomes "anesthetic" — as if one has had a local anesthetic injected. Some people are very adept at this, creating a sensation of numbness (i.e., translating any other sensation, such as a pinprick used for demonstration purposes, into a numb feeling) as if they had drawn on some sort of glove. Children respond very well to the concept of "the magic glove." One can then place the "anesthetized" hand on some other part of the body to which (s)he wishes to bring greater comfort, and let the sensation of numbness extend from the hand to that part of the body.

CHILDBIRTH

Settle yourself into hypnosis in your own way, very comfortably — good — and deepen your own level of hypnosis to the most useful level for you, today. Just nod your head or take a deep breath when you have arrived at that best level. *(Wait for the signal)*

(have the partner or labor coach there is possible)

Good. Now, take yourself FORWARD in time, easily and gently, to a date just a few *(days or weeks)* from now — I'm not sure just which date, and neither is your conscious mind — but your subconscious mind knows, and will take you there. And again, just let me know when you have arrived there. *(Wait for signal)* Good.

For many weeks now, you have been preparing for the birth of your baby. You have been practicing, and have acquired real skills in doing your own hypnosis. And now the time has

reinforcing her preparation

come, and you know that your baby is on its way. Perhaps you have had a little show, or your membranes have ruptured, or maybe your contractions are now in a definite pattern and are gradually getting closer and closer together, lasting longer, and becoming more intense.

setting the scene

This is a very exciting time, and that excitement is a very positive thing for you right now because the energy from that excitement will be part of your resources as your labor progresses.

use your voice to reflect what you are saying

It is a wonderful experience, having a baby, and it needs a lot of energy to really experience it in the most positive and rewarding way. So let that excitement be part of your own awareness right from the very beginning, and use it as a great resource as your labor continues.

positive expectations

You remember from our previous sessions, that labor occurs in three stages. The first stage allows the cervix to open by being drawn up into the uterus. The contractions, therefore, are especially designed by nature for that purpose. The next time you feel a contraction coming, think about its purpose; it is drawing up the cervix into the uterus in such a way that it opens more widely every time. As you understand how the contractions work, you will be able to accommodate your body more effectively to that mechanism.

shifting the emphasis to the *purpose* of the contractions instead of the discomfort

Remember that your body knows exactly what to do through this fascinating experience, and you can help *most effectively* by taking yourself away, a little distance away, each time you feel a contraction coming, so that your body can get on with its job.

pain relief through a dissociative technique

Practice that now. You will know when a contraction is beginning; use that as your signal, your cue. Let the beginning of each contraction be your cue. Your body and your subconscious mind will recognize that cue, even before your conscious mind is aware of it.

the body's activity is the mind's cue

Just to reinforce that even more usefully, I'll put my hand on your abdomen to symbolize that contraction. Yes, now—take yourself away, away when you feel that happening. Then, as it eases off *(lifting hand away),* bring yourself back again.

(physicians will feel comfortable doing this but psychologists may not—just adjust script accordingly—also a good reason for having someone else in the room)

You may want to go into hypnosis each time and then come out of it between contractions or you may choose to stay in a light level of hypnosis and deepen it with each contraction. You do whatever is right for you, using the beginning of each contraction as your signal—to go into hypnosis or to deepen your level of hypnosis and take yourself a little way away, a litle further, a little further away, a little further away, that's right, to some special place where you can rest and be comfortable while your body gets on with its job.

various ways to use hypnosis

further dissociation

It is almost as if you are watching yourself. Be very interested in what is going on, and appreciate what is happening within yourself: the cervix opening, the contractions designed specifically for that, and the cervix opening more and more, so each contraction becomes a little more forceful.

The uterus is a very strong muscle and the body *needs* that strength. It is workng hard! It is *laboring*. Let that energy help to take you a little further away and let that energy also help you respond most effectively. That's right.

using the resources referred to in the opening remarks

For most women with first babies, the cervix
opens about one centimeter every hour or so.
Of course, everyone is different and every
baby is special, and every labor is designed to
suit each particular set of circumstances, but
generally for first babies, it takes about an
hour, to open the cervix each centimeter.
It will be completely opened when it is 10
centimeters across from side to side.

As that time approaches now, the uterus   **labor is progressing**
begins to make little practices at pushing,
because the next stage of labor is to push the
baby down the birth canal, strongly but gently
to its birth. It feels as if everything is happen-   **"strongly but gently" —**
ing at once! Now is the time you need that   **distraction and mildly**
extra energy, that energy which comes from   **confusing**
your excitement, to go even *further* away,
because your body really needs to get on with   **deepening suggestions**
its job itself, and it can do that best when you
are away, further away, further away; and it
takes concentration and energy to take yourself
away because your body, and what is going
on in your body, is so much a part of your
awareness. Concentrate and stay away with
each contraction until the cervix is fully
opened. That's right. *(Your doctor or nurse)* will   **(change the wording if you**
tell you when your cervix has fully dilated.   **will be doing the delivery)**

Yes! You have reached that stage now. Now
things are changing quite dramatically, because
now the whole purpose of each contraction is
to push, guiding that baby, that special, special
baby down the birth canal to its birth; and so
now you have a different role to play. *Now,* each
time you *know* when a contraction is beginning.
When you recognize that, *go down into yourself,*   **new emphasis**
way down, right down deep within yourself,
and *be part of that force!* Add your strength and
energy to the strength of that contraction,

enjoying being part of that strength as that push carries your baby further down. Go WAY down within yourself, be part of that force; that's right, that's right.

Now, as each contraction wears off, r-e-a-l-l-y relax; gather up that strength and energy, getting ready for the next contraction. You have all the strength and energy that you need. In the time between contractions, restore and replenish yourself from within, and then, as once again you get the signal, go once more deep within yourself and add to that force.

The baby is now closer and closer to being born. Listen carefully to what *(your doctor or nurse)* is telling you, listen with your conscious and your subconscious mind. *(They)* will guide you in your pushing.

Now—the baby's head is being born; *stop pushing* so that *(they)* can ease the head gently into the world. You can use your breathing to accomplish that. Just breathe in a panting way for the rest of the contraction. You can do that.

Maybe you are watching in the mirror and if so, you can now see the baby's head. *(The doctor)* is wiping away a little mucus, clearing out baby's nose or mouth. Now, with this next contraction, once again push with all your energy as the shoulders and body are born— then—very quickly now!—there is your baby! There's your baby.

Reach down and hold your babe: look, see, touch, hear, smell—use ALL your senses, let all your senses rejoice as you get to know your baby, face to face now for the first time.

---

integrating; involving the woman actively; fosters bonding

reassurance

inner resources

breathing is a pain relief technique and is also used in prenatal classes (see "Breathing" p. 71)

speak softly but with great intensity

"use *all* of your senses"— invitation to multisensory imagery

And your baby gets to know you, because your baby can also feel, touch, hear your voice, even can see light and shadows. That baby is aware of the coolness of the room, the bright lights, the sounds—but most of all, your voice, your touch.

In a few minutes (*your doctor*) will ask you to give another little push, because it will be time for the third stage; time for the placenta to be delivered. You are so engrossed with your baby that you hardly even know what's happening, but now give that little push, and feel the placenta slide easily out from your body.

taking care of all the details

The nurse comes along and takes your baby for a few moments but only just a few feet away, and you can watch as she puts some ointment in the baby's eyes and gives it a small injection, to help its liver work more effectively in these early days. Then very soon you have your baby back in your arms.

preparing the mother that this will happen

(*The doctor*) may be finishing some suturing, taking care that everything is exactly how it should be with your uterus and vagina. You know that everything will heal very well, because your body is healthy. The uterus will contract back down to its usual size. That is called "involution." Your breasts are ready to produce milk, so even in these very early minutes and hours let baby begin to suck from your breast, because there are some very, very useful nutriments and protections for the baby in these early secretions.

posthypnotic suggestions for the postpartum period

Everything is exactly the way it should be for you both, as you get to know this very special new person in your life.

9

Chronic Pain Syndromes: A Choreography of Pain

As I mentioned in the earlier pages of this section, chronic pain syndromes have a special place in the realm of pain management.

They are considered notoriously difficult to treat and, indeed, they often are. Certainly, the usual approaches to pain relief often have litle effect. Medication is virtually useless for many sufferers. What is needed is a multifaceted approach that may include medication, nerve blocks, transcutaneous electrical stimulation, massage therapy, physiotherapy, behavioral modification, biofeedback and, often, psychotherapy and lifestyle counselling.

Add to this list hypnosis, acupuncture, and other altered states of consciousness (by whatever name you choose — visualization, relaxation response, etc). Don't forget deep prayer, which is extremely important for many people.

We have already said that hypnosis deals with changing the perception of pain. With chronic syndromes, we are dealing with two aspects: the perception of pain, certainly, but — more importantly — HOW THE PAIN INTRUDES INTO THAT PERSON'S LIFE.

Over the years I have learned to ask, when I am taking the history of a chronic pain sufferer, "Tell me how the pain intrudes into your life." So often their eyes will fill with tears; nobody had ever asked them that question, that way, before. But the *intrusion* IS the suffering, and the suffering component of pain is where we, with hypnosis, can help.

The second question I have learned to ask is: "Do you ever feel as if your whole life is now choreographed around this pain?" And it is. I have come to think of chronic pain as a sort of dissociative dance, and the dancing partners come from both within and without. So we begin to identify this choreography, and change the dance.

THE CHOREOGRAPHY

Let yourself ease into hypnosis now, as
you know so well how to do. Find your
most comfortable place in your body, and
use your breathing to spread that comfortable feeling right through your whole body.
That's right.

**already using a tried and
true pain-relief technique**

You remember that we had been talking
about an unusual metaphor for your pain:
we spoke of the *choreography* of that pain, and
you recognized that indeed, some aspects of
your life did seem to just revolve around
the pain as if there were no escape.

**the concept of using a
metaphor neutralizes any
negative interpretations
that somehow they are to
blame for their pain**

So let yourself settle even more comfortably
and begin to explore this metaphor. Let's see
what you can discover about this particular
dance. And then, how do you want to start
changing it?

**"discover...(the) dance"—
let your inflections support
the message**

First of all, find out who the dancers are. They
may be members of your family, friends, the
people at work, neighbors. All the people who,
in some way, are affected by OR affect this
chronic pain which has been with you for
so long.

**these are all the people in
one's life who somehow
could be contributing to
maintaining this choreography — often with the best
of intentions; but eventually
it turns sour, as the dance
seems to never end.**

Next, find out something even more
intriguing — what about the *inside* dancers?
Now, that's a different idea! What do you
make of that? Perhaps we can talk about it
after you come out of hypnosis but, for now,
find out what it means for YOU when I say,
"Who are the Inside Dancers?" I'll just be quiet
for a little time, to give you chance to explore
that idea. *(Be quiet for about 30 seconds)*

**of course the "inside
dancers" are the really
important ones: they may
find inside correlates of
the outside dancers — parts
of themselves that respond
to other persons' solicitude,
or anger, or depression**

Hmmm. Intriguing, as we said.

Now, there are others in this whole scenario whom we need to find out more about. First of all, who is the Director? Or is there more than one? And *who is the choreographer?* Maybe there's more than one of those, too.

continuing the metaphor: just who is directing this, anyway?

This can be the homework for your subconscious this time. Ask that wise deep inner part of your mind to find out some of this information that may be hidden from your thinking mind — although, of course, that part of your mind knows quite a lot about this, too — but invoke that inner wisdom to come forth. Then we can talk more about it next time, or you can work on it in your own self-hypnosis.

you don't need to do it all today — this is going to take a little time, and that's okay, that's appropriate.

reassurance for further work with you — the patient is not alone

Are you the choreographer? How are you going to change the dance?

but the one who does the changing is the patient

(Then bring the patient out of hypnosis in the way the two of you usually do.)

PART IV

PSYCHOSOMATIC DISORDERS

State of the Art

Hypnotic Approaches and Techniques

Fears and Phobias

10

State of the Art

Possibly no word is more misunderstood in medicine — by professionals and non-professionals alike — than "psychosomatic."

Quite simply, it means "mind and body." It does NOT mean "imaginary," "all in your head," "neurotic," or any of the other opprobrious connotations that are too often applied to it.

I have, in writing, this comment from a consultant physician to the family physician, who subsequently referred the patient for hypnosis: "How can we convince this woman that we have done all the investigations and her problem is *only psychosomatic*?" (emphasis mine). And another, from a Workers' Compensation Board physician: "This man thinks that he has a problem, but we think that he is the problem."

Both the patients referred to above responded well to hypnosis when their situation was reframed for them in this way:

> "It is impossible to be sick or injured and not have an emotional response to that; it is also impossible to be emotionally distressed — or overjoyed — and the body not respond to THAT. Therefore, when we say that something is 'psychosomatic,' we are simply stating the obvious — mind and body are interacting. Sometimes there is more input from the psyche, sometimes from the soma — but if one considers it in this way, EVERYTHING is 'psychosomatic.'
>
> "You can easily relate this to your own situation. Our job here is to explore your own resources, so that the input you are providing (the 'psyche' component) will guide you to an enhanced sense of well-being."

The whole field of *psychoneuroimmunology* attends to this; researchers like Ader (1993) and Pert (1993) are showing that there is literally NO separation of mind and body — both are present everywhere. One of the most important additions to the literature on psychosomatics is the book edited by Bill Moyers, *Healing and the Mind* (1993). It contains the transcripts from the exceptionally fine TV series of the same name.

Some things are difficult for us to comprehend; neuronal fibres are found in the immune system, for instance, or in the small intestine. It makes phrases such as "gut reaction" take on a whole new meaning (but then, at some subconscious level we already knew that, because that's how the phrase probably began— someone knew "more than (s)he knew that (s)he knew" about "body language").

Or the information that some of the stress hormones may actually contribute to the death of some brain cells, as reported on the same TV series by Felten (1993). Scary stuff, but absolutely fascinating and until we find out about it, we cannot deal with it. Luckily the research in this field is extensive (see bibliography). The answers are coming.

In the meantime, we soldier on. For your patients, avoid impossible promises and unrealistic expectations. State the irrefutable: the patient has far more resources than he/she realizes, and discovering more about these brings a greater sense of well-being.

11

Hypnotic Approaches and Techniques

BACK-TO-BEFORE

(The patient is already in hypnosis when this script begins, and has been considering the situation in some way. This is a useful pattern with which to end a session — knowing that further work will be done at the subconscious level before the next visit.)

In a few moments, you are going to feel my thumb on your forehead again and this time, when you feel it, I am going to invite your subconscious mind to begin taking a journey backwards in time — backwards in time, to the time BEFORE any of these distressing symptoms began. Indeed, even back to the time before any of the factors that contributed to those symptoms were there.

possibility of factors in childhood

And that may be far further back than you realize. It may even be back further than your conscious mind can follow.

gets your conscious mind off the hook

So let your conscious mind, do whatever it wants to do: it may wish to stay in THIS present — *(fill in the date)* — or it may go part of the way back in time, and watch (as it were) from a distance; or it may possibly go all the way back to where your subconscious mind has travelled. It will go where it is most comfortable, as that deeper, inner part of your

time dissociation

mind takes that journey backwards in time,
to the time before any of these feelings or
experiences or any of the contributing factors
are there.

And because your subconscious mind and
your conscious mind may be in different
times, you may find yourself experiencing
FEELINGS and wondering where they come
from. If that happens, you will know that they
come from where your *subconscious* mind has
taken you. So you can be entirely reassured
about that.

**the subject frequently
has somatic or emotional
responses for "no reason"**

reassurance

Enjoy becoming reacquainted with that
extremely pleasant and comfortable time: that
time when everything within you is functioning well and comfortably and effectively and
efficiently and you have that inner harmony
that will assure you of that.

**you *do* know what that is
like — "reacquainted"**

And everything between you and the outside
world is also harmonious, functioning well and
comfortably and effectively and efficiently and
you are happy and at peace, that great sense of
harmony both within and without.

(Allow a few moments for pleasant awareness)

Now turn your subconscious mind once more
to THIS present *(say the date)* and begin coming
forward in time, bringing those comfortable
feelings with it. And any time and every time,
along that journey, your subconscious mind
meets any factor that has in any way contributed
to those distressing symptoms, then let your
subconscious mind and your body TOGETHER
do whatever needs to be done to take care of
that factor. You know, when all the factors have
accumulated into one big problem, it sometimes

reassociating

**suggestions for clearing
away past intrusions and
interferences**

seems like an overwhelming task to make any
changes; but it is so much easier to deal with
just one factor. And in that way, in time, every
factor will be encountered, identified, and
taken care of, and you will be peaceful within
yourself, once again.

deal with one thing at a time

We do not know how long this journey is
going to take. At times it will go quickly —
there are just a few factors or they are easily
taken care of — or there may be times when
it goes much more slowly: there are many
factors or they are much more complex.
So we ask that one part of your subconscious
mind stay with this journey, take care of it,
monitor it.

the subconscious will take its own time

hypnotic logic

Then, in a few moments, when it is time to
come out of your hypnosis, all other levels of
your awareness, conscious and subconscious,
can return to their normal time and their
distinctly normal state.

important for the comfort of the patient; speak this paragraph very slowly and distinctly

(Close the session in your usual way.)

SYMPHONY METAPHOR

Sometimes I like to think of the body as
a symphony orchestra.

obviously particularly *à propos* for the musically inclined subject, but appreciated by many others also

A symphony orchestra makes beautiful
music; but it is made up of many sections
and each section is made up of many
instruments. As you know, sometimes an
instrument gets out of tune: a violin may
break a string or one of the reeds may need
to be cleaned. Something needs to be done
so that that instrument can produce beautiful
music again. Or sometimes, when working

there are many possible problems

on some composition, a whole section might
be having trouble with the rhythm or with a
difficult chord or harmonic, or the timing
might be off.

But despite the fact that an instrument may
need to be tuned or repaired or a whole section
might need to work on timing or rhythm, there
is nothing wrong with the *orchestra.* The orchestra
is still as strong and vital as ever. It is simply
that that instrument needs to be fixed, or that
section has to practice more, and when they
have done that then the orchestra is once again
harmonious, rhythmic, attuned to itself.

**by implication, nothing
wrong with the *person***

Well, the body is rather like that. If we think
of the body as being composed of many "sections"—the digestive system, the respiratory
system, the reproductive system, the cardiovascular system, the muscular system—all of these
systems make up the symphony that is the body.
And within each system, there are the various
"instruments": in the digestive system there are
the teeth and the mouth and the esophagus where
you swallow and the stomach and the sphincter
at the end of the stomach and the various parts
of the bowel; then there are also the auxiliary
organs like the liver. And all of these "instruments" make up that "section," just like the
instruments in the sections of the orchestra.

**one may change which
system is described to suit
a patient's symptomatology**

So, although attention may need to be paid
to one section or one instrument, yet the symphony—the body—is still wonderful, and still
has all the potential for making beautiful music.

Think to yourself, "My body is like a
symphony"—and feel the wonderful rhythms
of your body pulsing softly to their own special
beat within you, and harmony being restored.

completing the metaphor

INSOMNIA

I'm going to tell you about some ways in which you can use hypnosis to improve your sleep patterns.

People use hypnosis in a whole variety of ways to do that. Some people are so comfortable and relaxed in hypnosis that that relaxation just eases into sleep, and that's very nice indeed. Some people use hypnosis as a safe and comfortable place to wait for sleep to come, and that's very nice, too. You know that you can use that time in whatever way you wish. Some people just daydream; others take the opportunity of organizing or arranging something or clearing something away, looking forward to something—a safe and comfortable place to wait for sleep to come. Because, of course, in hypnosis, time loses its meaning, and so it is very comfortable to wait in hypnosis. An enjoyable, safe, protected place.

And then there are people who like to have some kind of specific pattern to encourage sleep, and some of those are really kind of interesting.

One pattern, for instance, is the blackboard technique.* It involves seeing (in your mind's eye) a blackboard; there is chalk there and clean brushes. You pick up the chalk in one hand and in the middle of the blackboard you put the numeral "1," making it very nicely.

That's right. Look at that for a few minutes, and then erase the "1" and up in the corner of the blackboard (I wonder which corner you'll choose?), up in the corner of the blackboard, you print the word "sleep"; and you look at that for a time, and then erase it.

new possibilities

it is alright to be awake *comfortably* awaiting sleep

alternative to clock-watching!

"those" can refer to the people or the pattern— deliberately vague (a bit of a confusion technique)

(*I first heard of this technique at an A.S.C.H. meeting years ago, but do not remember where or from whom)

suggestion of regression to school days; in childhood, sleep comes naturally

Now in the middle of the blackboard you put the numeral "2," enjoying the feeling in your hand as you write that — nice, flowing lines — that's right. You look at that and then you erase it and up in the corner of the blackboard, again, you print the word "sleep," and you look at that, and erase it.

kinesthetic imagery

reiterating "sleep"

And in the middle of the blackboard you print the numeral "3." I wonder how you'll make the "3"? With two half-circles, perhaps; I wonder if the upper one might be smaller or larger than the lower one, or the lower one smaller or larger than the upper one, or perhaps there is a straight line across the top, a straight line down diagonally, and then a curve — so many different ways to make the "3." Look at the one you have chosen, then erase it and up in the corner, print the word "sleep," paying particular attention to the "ee's" in "sleep" — that's right — and then erase it.

getting caught up in the imagery

"ee's" — drawn out to sound like "ease"

Then, in the middle of the blackboard you print the numeral "4." Do you make the "4" with open lines or a closed triangle? There are also many different ways of writing "4."

You continue this progression of printing a numeral and erasing it, and printing the word "sleep" and erasing it — then another numeral and erase it, and so on. You will be surprised to find yourself waking up in the morning! And it is always very interesting to think back on how many numerals one has written. It is very, very uncommon for people to have reached more than ten. You may be curious, if you decide to explore this particular approach, as to how many numerals you will have written before *you* find yourself waking up in the morning.

they must wake up in the morning to find out!

There are other specific techniques to invoke
and beckon sleep. For instance, sometimes it's
kind of fun to find out how many words you
can think of that have something to do with
sleep and to spend time in hypnosis remembering those, thinking of words like sleep,
sleeping, sleeper, drowsy, slumber, dream,
dreamy, sometimes words like cozy, quilt,
pillow, all the words you can think of that
have something to do with sleep. That's
kind of a game to play.

**childhood games —
regression again to time
when sleep was natural**

For some folks, it is really more enjoyable to
do something challenging, like adding up long
columns of figures or finding out how many
words you can make from Constantinople —
those sorts of games.

Some people just enjoy wandering through
a wonderful pathway where there are little
side paths that take you to delightful places;
and each place the pathway takes you to, has
something very comfortable to do with sleep.
One path might take you to a hammock, for
instance; another path might take you to a
basket where a kitten is sleeping; another
might take you to your favorite bedroom
when you were just a little girl *(boy)*, where
you went to sleep and dreamt wonderful
dreams. Things like that, with each little
path, each little byway taking you to a special
place that has something very special to do
with sleep. You can ask your subconscious
to lead you to those places, in your hypnosis,
so you could enjoy, over the next few weeks
or months, exploring *all* these various
possibilities and finding out which ones
work best for you, adding your own special
inner knowledge to make those approaches
very personal for you.

daydreaming at night

**invitation to use their
ingenuity**

**once more, back to
childhood**

Just a word now about waking up in the middle of the night. Often, when one wakens in the middle of the night, one of the very best things to do is to get up and do something that you love doing — a hobby, something that you really enjoy: crossword puzzles, jigsaws, knitting, making jewellery, writing poetry — and promise yourself that you will spend at least a half-hour doing that before going back to bed, at least half an hour. Promise yourself that you will do that for at least half an hour, really enjoying doing something that you really love to do, that you hardly ever get time in the daytime to do. Then when you go back to bed, you can know that you have had that special time by yourself, for yourself, and you can fall gently back to sleep remembering how delightful that was.

reassuring that this can be a *good* experience

There are many ways in which you can use your hypnosis to approach sleep comfortably and to enjoy every moment of that sleeping.

Go backward in time, now, to childhood — that time in your life when sleep was so natural, so easy, that you simply took it for granted.

definite suggestion for time regression at this time

You see, you know a lot about sleeping. Your body *knows* how to sleep — it has known how to sleep since before you were born! Let your body and your subconscious mind become reacquainted with that deep inner knowledge. Your conscious mind, your thinking mind, can do whatever it wants to do, while your subconscious mind and your body renew this old acquaintanceship. You may be aware of some of the warm cozy feelings that that renewal evokes — you can be very interested in those feelings, in your own awareness. Just let the feelings flow by, easily and gently. That's right.

"the person has, within him, the information and knowledge that he needs..."

kinesthetic "memories"

We know that all patterns begin for a purpose; so, for some reason, some reason that may still remain a mystery to your *conscious* mind, your inner, deeper mind thought that you had to stay awake, or sleep very, very lightly. Maybe it still thinks so. Maybe it is doing its best to keep that pattern for you because it still thinks that it is needed!

validation

avoiding guilt or blame

Tell your subconscious mind, and your body, that it is alright now to let that old, interrupted sleep pattern go, to be finished and put away, and that you now need a new, comfortable sleep pattern for the present and for the future.

opportunity for conclusion and new beginning

Perhaps, in time, it will be alright for your subconscious mind to comfortably let you be aware of what that old necessity was. For now, enjoy the beginning of a new, useful pattern, and look forward to refreshing, restoring, replenishing sleep, *every* night.

possibility of further clarification without remaining stuck in the old pattern

REHEARSE SUCCESSFUL RECOVERY

In the past weeks, as we have been working together, you have learned a great deal about your body and how mind and body work together.

positive reinforcement for work done

You have also learned how great your influence on your body can be, when the subconscious and the body communicate and share information.

the person's *own* contribution is the most important

You know, also, how vitally important it is to give your body the positive MESSAGE about regaining health. We are going to give some of those positive messages today in a very simple, practical, and useful way.

Settle yourself down even more comfortably, and ease to whatever level of hypnosis is just right for you at this time, to achieve what you are going to achieve today. That's right.

positive expectation of achievement

We have already, in previous sessions, spent some time considering the past, and how you got to where you are now, in order to finish with that past and put it comfortably and securely AWAY.

the way has been prepared

And we have also spent some useful time on the present: what you can be and are doing to promote recovery and regain your sense of vitality and well-being.

past and present linked

So it seems appropriate, today, to go *into the future:* into the future, to the time when you are SO MUCH BETTER, and to enjoy that promise of good things to come.

in trance, going into the future is perfectly logical

When you feel my thumb on your forehead, then, take yourself *forward* in time, this time, to the time when you are feeling so much better and your symptoms (*you may wish to specify which symptoms*) have subsided. You have achieved your goal — regaining that sense of well-being in mind and body.

". . . forward in *time*, this *time,* to the *time.* . ." — repetitions of the word to further promote time dissociation

expectation *has been achieved*

Enjoy experiencing, once again, that vitality and energy. Let all your awarenesses be part of that — mind, body, and spirit. See yourself, hear yourself, feel yourself enjoying life, engaging in all those activities that you remember so well and are once again renewing.

bringing past and future together — this is another instance of blurring time definitions in hypnosis

Think of your very favorite pastime — a hobby, or walking along the seawall or through a cool glen; or perhaps dancing or sharing a social time with friends. Think of being back to work, knowing that you are doing a good job because now you are well again and can really concentrate without the distractions of those old symptoms that beset you for so long. What a wonderful feeling!

affirmation imagery ("a statement about the future...")

Spend some time in that future present, just experiencing and completely immersing yourself in that time. Every moment that you are there, you are sending strong, positive messages to yourself—to your subconscious mind, and thence to your body. Visit that future present often in the next few days and weeks, in your own hypnosis at home.

"Future present"— a grammatical term converted into hypnotic language: "be present in the future"

Every time you do so, you will reaffirm and strengthen your own power to be well. You are REHEARSING SUCCESSFUL RECOVERY!

For now, it is time to leave there and come back to *this* present, *(say the date).* And when you are again fully back in this room, bring yourself up out of your hypnosis in your own way.

reassociating time frames, anchoring the date

PRIMARY FUNCTION OF THE BRAIN

Think, for a moment, about the functions of the brain.

Such an incredible organ. We can scarcely comprehend all of its myriad functions.

But it is interesting, in view of the work we have been doing lately, to spend a few moments today, thinking about the *primary* function of the brain.

Usually, we think that the primary function of the brain is to think. But really, it is only the *thinking* part of the brain that thinks that.

a little joke at the expense of the conscious mind

In reality, the primary function of the brain is to *keep us alive and well:* to take care, to attend to those thousands of biochemical and hormonal balances that require constant monitoring, constant reevaluation, and adjustment. THAT has been the primary function of the brain, for millenia — ever since life came upon this earth.

the deeper functions of the brain are vital (literally)

keeping alive and well is much more important than thinking

To keep us alive and well — to maintain *homeostasis* — equilibrium within.

This basic function of the brain is achieved through many routes, and one of the most important is the communication between the subconscious mind and the body. This is the route, the pathway by which we can and do influence our bodies and their functioning. When you give the message to your deep inner mind that your body is once again to achieve harmony and balance, you are inviting your brain to fulfill its most basic function — that maintenance of homeostasis: keeping you alive, and well.

inviting the thinking part of the mind to collaborate

Mind and body are, of course, really one. But it is a useful concept to think of them as *communicating* and, therefore, to have communication pathways.

We know a great deal about these pathways — they can be through biochemicals, hormones, or nerve pathways. One of the paths that we know best, that there has been MUCH research about, is the path through the part of the brain known as the limbic system. This path goes from the idea or thought in the thinking part

although it may seem that the following is far too technical, I have found that almost all patients have been able to understand it

of the brain—the conscious—to the deeper parts of the brain—the subconscious—by the microscopic neuronal fibres; thence through the most mature part of the brain, the part called the hypothalamus, where the limbic system is found.

> very well, and appreciate the explanation—which they then process in their own way, making it personal and meaningful for them

The limbic system is VERY, VERY important to us because of the wonderful tasks that it performs. For instance, emotion is processed there. We know, and *you know, too,* how much our feelings can affect us. Sometimes such feelings can overwhelm us, and even make us feel quite sick.

> this is why the emotional content of imagery is so important

> everybody relates to this

So this important pathway passes through the limbic system and then by biochemical messenger across to the pituitary gland, the granddaddy gland of the body. The pituitary gland then sends out its hormones to all the other glands in the body, such as the adrenals, the thyroid, and the ovaries.

AND THEN THE BODY SENDS MESSAGES BACK!! Right along the same pathways. We always must remember that mind-body communication is a two-way street.

> most important!

So this is how your brain, your wonderful brain, fulfills its primary function—to keep you alive, and well.

HEALING IMAGERY

All living things in the plant and animal world have one thing in common: all have within them, the most incredible capacity to HEAL. If you simply think of a wounded animal, or

a damaged plant, you can affirm that
statement for yourself. Animals—man
included—recover from wounds and illness;
the plant grows new leaves or branches, and
sometimes even has scars to remind the
observer that once, it was wounded.

universality of the
capacity to heal

You also have this wonderful capacity. You
also have this miraculous healing energy
within you.

Go now, deep within yourself: to the very
center of yourself, to the source of that healing
energy within you. Go to the very source of
that healing energy; be aware of that energy
that comes from the very center of yourself.
Gather up that energy, and *direct it to that part
of your body where you instinctively know it must
be directed!*

invitation to go deeper
into trance

you can trust your
intuition

Each one of us has his or her own personal
concept of that energy. For me, it is a source
of light—a source of healing light, like the sun,
a light that can be directed to the part of the
body that needs healing, and suffuse that part
of the body with its healing glow. It is a golden
light, that surrounds and bathes the ill or
wounded part of the body with that healing
golden energy.

everyone's concept is right
for him or her

Discover YOUR own concept of what your
healing energy is. Locate it deep within you,
and direct it to wherever your body needs it.

Now FEEL, *sense* the healing that is already
beginning within you. You can actually FEEL
that healing. *Feel the healing, while you heal the
feeling.* That's right. Direct that energy through
your body, to wherever you intuitively know
it is needed—knowing that you may even be

hypnotic language that
appeals particularly to
the kinesthetic imager

surprised at the part of your body that you have intuitively chosen! But knowing, also, that the subconscious mind has so much more information than the conscious mind has, the subconscious mind may know that some *other* part of the body, different from where your conscious mind would have thought, may need that healing first. Trust your subconscious mind to direct that energy; trust your intuitive response.

opportunity for intuitive input

positive suggestion for healing

but generally better to let the subconscious to that itself

Now let your wonderful, creative imagination formulate an image, in your awareness, of what that ill or wounded part of your body is like — what it looks like, or feels like (kinesthetically or tactilely), or indeed even sounds like — discordant, harsh, hoarse, a grating sound perhaps, or thin and reedy with little substance.

emphasizing the importance of self-trust

This image could be pictorial, as if you were looking at an anatomy book; or in three dimension, like a piece of sculpture. It could be entirely symbolic, or graphic. Use your own talents to devise an image that has meaning for YOU.

formation of images using all the senses; images must have personal meaning to be effective

Use all of your sensory awarenesses to formulate that image. Fill that image with all the detail you possibly can — what you see, hear, feel, touch, taste, smell. Remember color, and strength.

invoking all the senses

Then place that image, in your inner awareness, on one side.

Now, begin to create another image: this image is of healing, of convalescence, of recovery. It is the image of what your body will be like — will look like, feel like, sound like when you are well again; restore harmony to

your body, and power. Fill in all of THAT
wonderful detail, in whatever kind of image
is right for you, remembering that the image
can be realistic or symbolic, two- or three-
dimensional, whatever you instinctively   **ego-strengthening**
know is congruent with your deep sense
of self.

Place this image beside the earlier one.

Your task now becomes very simple: you   **simple expectation of**
simply need to evolve the first image into   **success**
the second.

Some people like to do this in a way similar to
rifling through those little pictures in the upper
corners of comic books — flipping the pages
quickly so that the cartoons seem to move;
some choose to make a video or movie of the   **triggers for the imagination**
process; some draw intermediate images —
short-term goals, as it were; some just sense
the evolution of one into the other.

In your own hypnosis every day, reinforce
this healing imagery. The more frequently
you do that, the stronger the message that
you are giving to your subconscious mind   **affirmations in imagery**
and thence to your body: I CAN BE WELL:
I AM ALREADY ON THE ROAD TO
RECOVERY!

HEALING IMAGERY — OTHER TECHNIQUES

1. Color

Another type of imagery uses color extensively and gives it priority. Some
people paint a picture in their imaginations — a picture in the colors of illness and
disease. The healing imagery, then, involves painting a new picture, using the
colors of health, or in changing the existing (in the mind's eye) picture as
convalescence and healing ensue.

A variation is to simply perceive colors—in the shades and tones of woundedness or ill health—swirling about in various patterns; gradually the colors change, merging into the vibrant colors of full recovery.

One thinks of this type of imagery with the artistically inclined (not necessarily artists).

2. Music

For those who use auditory imagery more extensively, music can be used to great advantage. The music of disease may be perceived as jarring and discordant—each subject will have his or her own ideas about that; many will hear (with their inward ear) a specific piece of music that fits their interpretation. The music may change suddenly or gradually, "letting it happen" or deliberately ending one and beginning another.

Pain which is perceived in auditory terms—e.g., throbbing—may be altered in this way, changing the image of the pain as the music changes *(see also Hypnotic Techniques for Pain Relief, p. 67)*. Personally, I have changed Heavy Metal (a throbbing ankle with torn ligaments) to a Mozart opera with great success! Similarly, musical representations of illness may change to those of health and happiness.

These musical metaphors may be combined with the frequent use of words such as harmony, rhythm, attuned, tempo, etc. *(see also Symphony Metaphor, p. 89).*

3. Wind, Breezes

The image of a soft breeze wafting away illness, bringing strength and a sense of well-being, is very pleasant. A brisk wind, blowing disease away is more active and invigorating for some.

Alternatively, the concept of a storm, even a raging gale, as the terrifying or devastating illness, subsiding to a warm, healing breeze bringing peace and comfort may describe some patients' situation more vividly.

4. Healing water

This could be, figuratively, swimming in a magic pool or immersing oneself in some sort of healing water. We sometimes talk of "taking the waters," referring to a spa or health resort. In that case, the healing water is taken "within," rather than "without."

Case History

D.M., a little boy of six years, had one of the worst cases of eczema I've seen in a child. He was highly allergic to many things—foods, pollens, some clothing materials—and every allergic response exacerbated the eczema.

He had been missing a great deal of school (this was England, where they go to school earlier than in North America) and was showing some behavioral problems that were not hard to understand, but nevertheless were a cause for anxiety.

No medication seemed to help very much, even steroids—and his parents were unhappy about the amount of steroids that he was taking (especially with so little positive effect).

When I saw him he was a listless child, lying on the couch in a darkened room even though it was a pleasant summer day. He was so very apathetic that I wondered whether he would engage with me, but he did. He also, like other children I have come across, was intrigued with the thought that maybe HE could do something that the doctors couldn't do. (Perhaps it is a common response from the child in all of us!)

He went into hypnosis easily, as children almost always do. I encouraged him to find his own imagery and, with a little prompting, he did. It was twofold: he had a friendly dragon named David, who protected him, and he and David liked to bathe in a wonderful river—a very special, magic river where the water washed away all the irritation and discomfort in his skin and brought healing.

I saw him only that one time, although I spent about an hour and a half with him, playing hypnosis games. He always came back to David, and the magic healing river.

Much to my delight, some time after I got back to Canada I received a letter from his mother and a postcard from him. The postcard told me that he and David still played all the time in the river. His mother told me that the improvement was remarkable, and he seemed like a different child emotionally, too. (No wonder!)

D.M. kept in touch with me for about two years, sometimes sending a postcard in a letter from his mother, sometimes just sending it himself. His eczema continued to improve, he was back to school, and David the Friendly Dragon continued to protect him and play with him in the magic river.

Healing water also has some reference to the safety of the womb, when one is floating in the warm amniotic fluid. The link to baptism, or being "born again," is another possibility to explore with some patients. Obviously, one chooses the metaphor very carefully. A good history is the first essential, rapport a close second.

Healing imagery has an infinity of variations. Use your own creative imagination to present wonderful options to your patients.

INFLUENCING THE MIND/BODY CONNECTION

(The patient in this script has been suffering from chronic post-viral fatigue syndrome which started with an upper respiratory infection two years before.)

Today we are going to discuss, in more detail, some of the many ways in which mind and body work together. It is a truly miraculous partnership, and one that we can utilize even more fully, in hypnosis.

recognizing the importance and offering better opportunity for success

Get very comfortably settled, then, in your own way taking yourself a little further into hypnosis to that level which you instinctively know is just right for you at this time. You know that you *can always change* your level of hypnosis — deeper or lighter — *whenever that change would be useful* for you.

"you can always change . . . . . . whenever that change would be useful . . ."; **multilevel meaning — alter vocal tone accordingly**

Turn your attention to your own body, now, and to what has been happening to it during these past two years. It has been a very distressing and discouraging time; now you feel within yourself that you are beginning to get well again. We want to foster that process by encouraging your mind and body to work together in the most positive way.

stating the fact

respect intuition

how to proceed

We have talked about the fact that chronic stress depresses the immune defenses of the body, and these past two years certainly have been stressful for you. So we will begin by focusing on your body's immune system.

validating the long illness

Go even further within yourself now, to the very center of yourself, and ask your subconscious mind and your body to communicate, *each giving the other the information that it needs* for your immune defenses to become strong and

the communication is always BIDIRECTIONAL (Rossi, 1986)

vital again. Your subconscious mind and your body TOGETHER can communicate, collaborate, cooperate to do *whatever needs to be done* to achieve that return to strong healthy function.

communicate, collaborate, cooperate — alliterative emphasis

That's right. FEEL that communication occurring, on your deepest intuitive level. Good. Very, very good. As your defenses become stronger and stronger, you know that you are protected from further infection, and so you can direct more energy to healing and restoring within your body.

kinesthetic awareness

good things are happening which lead to more good things

Strength begins to return to your muscles; your appetite improves and you sleep better.

Ask your subconscious mind and your body to communicate on all these aspects, also, during your own hypnosis time every day, and in the same way, to do WHATEVER NEEDS TO BE DONE to achieve this return to health. Add your own healing imagery to this practical and effective convalescent program.

the subconscious and body together know what needs to be done; you can further the process with healing imagery

And with healing comes a lifting of those feelings of depression. You *know* that you are getting better, and it is wonderfully reassuring to know that.

the process continues

Everything we say, or think; everything we FEEL, every emotion; how we behave, and why we behave that way — all of these are directly translated into some response within the body. This is vital information for us when we are considering mind/ body communication.

mind/body communication

Therefore let yourself become *even more aware* of your thoughts and words and actions; and if you discover, for instance, that you are speaking in a negative way ("I don't feel well"), then you

suggestion for deepening now as well as greater awareness later

can change that immediately to a positive
statement ("I'll feel better tomorrow"). This
reinforces for your subconscious mind, the   **how to utilize**
message that POSITIVE is what you intend.

Best of all is the knowledge that your mind and
body are working together, a true partnership;
and that you can enhance that partnership   **you are important!**
through your own resources and your own
hypnosis every day.

MIND/BODY COMMUNICATION — GENERAL SUGGESTIONS

There are some very general suggestions for mind/body communication that can
be incorporated into many of the scripts for healing and/or understanding the
psychosomatic concepts that are fundamental for recovery.

For instance, there is a section in *"Primary Function of the Brain"* (pp. 97–99) that
is adaptable in many cases. Further suggestions are found in *"Influencing the Mind/
Body Connection"* (pp. 105–107), and in *"State-Dependent Learning"* (pp. 108–109).

Much of this is based on the work of Ernest Rossi (1986) and elaborated by
him and David Cheek (Rossi & Cheek, 1988).

Another useful suggestion is the following concept:

> You can think of the communication between your mind and your body as being
> part of a triangle: the top of the triangle can be thought of as the brain, the
> conscious mind; then, on the left-hand side of the base we have the subconscious,
> and on the right-hand side, the body.
>
> Communication occurs along ALL sides of this triangle between conscious and
> subconscious, between conscious and the body, and between the subconscious
> and the body. All are important, but *the most important is the communication across the
> base,* the *subconscious/body* connection.
>
> This is the connection that is strengthened in your hypnosis, and why it is impor-
> tant to do your hypnosis every day.
>
> And remember, the communication goes both ways. There are no one-way streets
> in this land — just wonderful sharing of information, communication, back and
> forth, along all sides of this triangle. Conscious, thinking mind; subconscious,
> emotional mind; sensate, experiencing body.
>
> YOU.

To give a reinforcing posthypnotic suggestion that will enhance these mind/body communication concepts, you might say:

> And you can ask your mind and your body to continue this communication, to collaborate and cooperate towards achieving your healing and recovery.

> And you can reinforce this for yourself many times throughout the day by just repeating this little mnemonic: "M-B—C-C-C." That's right, you can make it into a little jingle: *"M-B—C-C-C."* *M*ind/*B*ody Communication, *C*ollaboration, *C*ooperation. Say it to yourself many times a day, whenever you think of it, whatever you might be doing at the time.

> "M-B—C-C-C." Many times, every day.

STATE-DEPENDENT LEARNING

(Patient is in hypnosis)

We have talked several times about the fact that everything we say, think, feel and how we behave is directly translated into some physiological response within the body. Such responses may be very noticeable, or hardly noticeable at all, but they are there. The biochemical and hormonal interactions are very complex, but it is enough for us to know that they exist.

There is another important aspect to that fact. Such responses are *learned responses*.

In any situation, we can consider our response to it, whatever it might be, as something that we have learned. And the *state* that we are in while we are engaged in that *learning* process, the emotional and stress-related state, is a vital ingredient in the lesson.

defining the term: "state. . .learning"

a vital ingredient, because the emotional component is the best access for change through hypnotic intervention (Rossi, 1986)

Because of the essential nature of that combination, whenever we are back in that emotional state, we tend to reinforce the learned response, and the responding reinforces the emotional state.

Understanding this link gives us another focus for healing intervention. With this aspect firmly in mind, we can ask mind and body to communicate, collaborate, and cooperate, and to do WHATEVER THEY NEED TO DO to modify that learned response into one that is now *suitable for our new needs*. That may involve changes in the response, or the emotional state, or both.

we do not need to specify WHAT needs to be done; in fact, it is probably much more useful to phrase it this way — then we do not presume to know more than the subconscious does

Recognition of the state-dependency element and of the decision to change is the key.

Apply this now to your own situation. Think back to the time when all this began; how you felt at that time, what was happening in your life, the various stresses that you had; what were things like when this illness began?

motivation is very important; making it personal

Then, begin to put the pieces of the puzzle together, using this concept of the *state* of things to add to your evaluation. Ask your subconscious mind to gather information for you, over the next few days, that will be useful in this regard. You could be astonished at what you might recognize or remember. Then, with this added information, you will have a better understanding of your body's reactions.

more information

It is very difficult to change something when you are lacking some of the information. Now that you know more about it, positive change can occur more easily and successfully.

further reason to expect success

12

Fears and Phobias

Therapists differ in their approach to fears and phobias. Some feel that the patient must find the "real" source of the fear — or at least the perceived "real source" — and analyze it and/or "work it through" before somehow consigning it to the realm of comfortable memories.

Others feel it is appropriate just to deal with the symptoms, and the source will take care of itself.

Patients differ also, in similar directions, but most of all they want RELIEF. If we always bear that in mind and use our interviewing skills to find out which approach is most appropriate for which patient, then we can truly offer a variety of possibilities which the *patient* can use to best advantage.

DE-FUSING PANIC

I am going to describe for you a way in which you can have some tools immediately available to you for relieving an anxiety attack.

"immediately available" sounds good to any panic sufferer!

You know how miserable it is to all of a sudden feel that coming on; so, to have some sort of band-aid, as it were, that you could immediately use to relieve that feeling — that is very, very comforting. I'm going to describe such a situation.

In order to learn how to do that, I suggest that here, now, while you are very safe here in my office in hypnosis, you allow yourself to feel

arranging the safe framework

110

what one of those attacks feels like; *but* you can limit the feeling to just however much is okay for you to feel at this time.

Hypnosis is wonderful, you know, because you can make those restrictions. You're safe here in my office; just let yourself feel what one of those panic attacks feels like, knowing that you can limit those feelings to just whatever is okay, whatever feels manageable. That's right.

But whatever feels okay, let yourself feel that amount to the fullest, and take particular note of what happens first. Maybe the first thing you feel is a little fluttering in your chest, or your tummy; perhaps you notice your breathing is changing or your heartbeat is changing. Some people feel a little tension in the head, or your tummy is growling; maybe your hands become moist.

all people with panic attacks have some, if not most, of these symptoms; this reassures the subject that you do know how he or she feels

Just let yourself feel your own personal complex of feelings for those situations, remembering that you can limit it to just whatever feels okay for you to feel here, knowing that you are safe. But whatever is okay, let yourself feel that much to the *fullest.*

trance logic: "just feel a little...but feel it to the *fullest*"

Then when you reach the very fullest of that amount, whatever it is, hold that—just hold it—ahh, good for you. Now, bit by bit and one at a time, reverse EACH SYMPTOM. Start with your breathing. Breathing is something that we can deliberately change and regulate, so it is perhaps the best place to start. Let your breathing ease back, just concentrate on your breathing—that's the idea, you know how to do it, that's right.

watch your subject carefully—*your* timing is important

As your breathing comes back into the comfortable zone again, you'll notice that your heartbeat is already beginning to do that, too, because breathing and heartbeat go together. When your breathing is comfortable again, wait a little longer; and when your heart rate feels comfortable again, then choose the next one — maybe that fidgetty feeling in your hands, or maybe releasing the knot in your tummy — that's the idea; in the back of the neck there now — that's right, releasing each one by itself in turn until everything is back to normal again. See? You know exactly where to put your hands. That's it. When everything is easy again, then let yourself settle back down again, take a deep breath and settle back down comfortably in the chair.

this patient moved her hands to her neck for comfort; always utilize whatever the patient does, in a positive way

Just think of what you have learned in these last few minutes. You've learned at least two very important things: one is that you know exactly what to do with your hands, exactly where to put them, and exactly where that place is in your neck; you know exactly what to do, where to focus your attention.

ego-strengthening

The second thing you have learned is that *you can do it!* You have reversed each part of that symptom complex. Isn't that wonderful! I knew you could, and you've just proven it.

positive reinforcement — the subject is doing it right

Now just to reinforce that, go through it again, again restricting the feeling to only what is okay to feel this morning right here in my office in hypnosis. You may feel comfortable about feeling a little more this time, because you know you can do it, but whatever is okay with you, limit it to that, that's right, and whatever is okay, let yourself feel that to the fullest, yes, that's right, that's right, that's it — hold it right there.

once having done it, the subject will be more comfortable (and trusting) about doing it again

Then, when you are feeling it to the fullest
once again, one by one, reverse each part in
turn, usually starting with the breathing
because it is something that we can have such
definite control over; breathing comes first,
then you yourself know how to proceed — the
back of your neck, right in the pit of your
stomach, that's right. One by one, it is
important to do it one by one.

**she again used her
hands — on her neck,
then her abdomen**

That's it. Then, when everything is back to
normal again, you can settle comfortably back
in the chair, taking a deep breath. That's
right. Just take care of that last feeling in the
pit of your stomach. It's interesting, isn't it? —
the way the feelings have a sort of a pattern.
That's right, that's better — that shimmering
feeling just letting you know that your muscles
are relieving their tensions. That's good.

**the patient gave a little
movement**

And then, when you are ready, breathe a very
deep breath. What a relief! And just settle
right back down. That's right.

**taking a deep breath and
letting it out always
relieves muscle tension**

Congratulations! You see, you've done it twice
and you've done it extremely well. And now
you know that you have something you can
do immediately, if ever you get stuck.

Next time, of course, we are going to be
talking about *preventing* it happening at all, but
it is so comforting to know that you have something that you can do immediately — just like
having that band-aid handy. Something you
can do right away, wherever you may be; one
by one, reverse each part of that symptom
complex, usually starting with the breathing
because that is something that we can deliberately control. And then, within a very short
time (as you can tell), the symptoms ease away

positive reinforcement

band-aid in place!

reassurance of further work

and you are back in perfect control again—
in fact, YOU ARE IN CONTROL THE
WHOLE TIME THAT YOU ARE RE-
VERSING THAT SYMPTOM COMPLEX!
Isn't that wonderful! Yes, you can regain
control that quickly. That's marvellous.

**handing the control back
to the subject**

Next time we'll talk about preventing it
happening. In the meantime, you know
now that there is always something that
you can do, right away. That's good.

PROGRESSIVE-RETROGRESSIVE TECHNIQUE

In the past few sessions, you have been
acquiring more and more information about
how and why the fears that you felt when you
thought of going somewhere on an airplane
started.

This has been very useful information for
you and you have been able to reevaluate old
experiences from the past that were interfering
with the present.

Now, however, it is time to look ahead, to
the future; so take yourself a little further
into hypnosis, to that level that is just right
for you today, and as you are doing that, take
yourself also FORWARD in time, to the time
when you have successfully completed your
first comfortable airplane journey. It is
perhaps half an hour after you have arrived
at your final destination, and you are sitting
down with a cup of tea or some refreshment,
thinking back over that very, very positive
experience. You feel so *satisfied,* so pleased
with yourself—as, indeed, you have every
right to feel.

a new approach

presumption of success

Savor that feeling for a little longer. Really
enjoy that. That's right — it's a great
feeling.

Now, begin coming backwards in time
towards the present, to the time when the
plane has just landed — and Oh! what a
feeling — what an absolutely *wonderful* feeling!
That sense of jubilation, of VICTORY!
"I'VE DONE IT!! I've *done* it." Ohhh.

**"backwards in time
towards the present" —
a time confusion technique**

Now, backwards in time again towards the
present, to the time when the flight is three-
quarters over. You feel great — you KNOW,
absolutely and without any doubt, that the rest
of the flight will be successful, because it has
been so successful all the way through. You
are filled with happiness.

**pause between each
segment, to allow time to
appreciate the feelings**

Now, backwards in time again, to the time
when you look at your watch and realize that
the flight is more than half over. Amazing!
How could the time have gone so quickly and
comfortably? This IS success — you sense it
deep within yourself.

**landmarks in the
journey — the person is
"remembering the future"**

Then, backwards in time again, to the time
when you are about a quarter of the way into
the flight and you're feeling very encouraged,
because it IS going well; you are feeling
comfortable, and at ease — quite different from
previous flights. This *is* going to be alright, as
you had sensed that it would be.

And once more backwards in time, now,
to the time when you have just boarded that
airplane, and are getting yourself settled into
your seat; there is a calmness within you that
is extremely pleasant. "I will succeed." You say
it quietly but very positively to yourself.

And backwards in time just once more, to the time when you are on your way to the airport, or just checking in. You have a sense of determination within yourself that is different from previous flights. Yes, there IS something different, this time.

arriving back at the present, he now knows how he got to the victorious future

And so you board the plane, and get yourself settled, recognizing a calmness within yourself that is extremely pleasant. "I will succeed." You say it quietly but very positively to yourself.

When you are about a quarter of the way into the flight, you are feeling very encouraged, because it IS going well, you ARE feeling comfortable and at ease, it IS different from previous flights and it IS going to be alright — in fact it *is* alright.

(as the journey now progresses *forward*, use the same words and phrases, as much as possible, to refer to the earlier "backwards" journey; this offers even more time dissociation)

And soon, it seems very soon, you look at your watch and realize that the flight is more than half over. Amazing! How could the time have gone so quickly and comfortably? This IS success — you sense it deep within yourself.

And just a little while later, the flight is three-quarters over; you feel great, knowing absolutely and without any doubt that the rest of the flight will be successful. You are filled with happiness.

And now — the plane has landed! And Oh! WHAT a feeling — that sense of jubilation — "I'VE DONE IT!! I've done it."

Victory Reassured!

And, when you have arrived at your final destination and you are sitting down, thinking back over that very, very positive experience, there is a sense of satisfaction deep within you that you know you will now always have. You are proud to be you.

OTHER TECHNIQUES

1. Comforting the Child Within

An adaptation of this technique (see p. 110) is frequently an invaluable mechanism for easing the root of many fearful or phobic situations. One asks the patient to experience — while he is safe in hypnosis in your office — the fear; then, to go back to the time when he *first felt that FEELING.* Emphasize that the situation will in all probability be totally different from what triggers the fear or panic now, but the FEELING will be the same. One is creating an "affect bridge."

Almost always, the child will have been (or thought that he was) alone, lost, abandoned, smothering, etc. Ask the adult, then, to go back and comfort the child — explain, reassure, soothe. Often, just one session, using this technique, will improve the condition dramatically, but I usually reinforce it at the next session.

I also delay using this approach until the patient has some resources in place, such as the "de-fusing panic" technique.

2. Desensitization

Utilizing the hypnotic state as a safe place to go through a desensitization procedure can be useful in some cases. One could invite the person to find a tiny picture of the phobic object in an imaginary book, for instance; then find bigger pictures, then image the object itself behind glass, etc.

13

Daydreams for Discovery

The richest lode for finding therapeutic nuggets must surely be in the realm of metaphor, fantasy, and other forms of imagery.

Both directed and undirected fantasy can be useful. Music offers great healing potential; it often induces a trance state spontaneously and the harmony in sound somehow becomes directly translated into emotional and physiological harmony as well.

The various metaphors presented here are certainly directed. To the critical, thinking mind, the symbolism is pretty obvious. But the subconscious mind is wiser; it knows that these directed "daydreams" DO bring the invitation to explore and discover, at much subtler and more personal levels, the inner resources that each of us has stored away, and it puts aside critical evaluation in favor of the richer potential.

Hence — enjoy your daydreams, and discover your inner wealth.

MOUNTAIN METAPHOR

This fantasy begins, as many do, in a meadow — a beautiful, beautiful meadow on a lovely golden day; the sort of day that sometimes comes at the end of summer. You think summer is over and the autumn wind and rain are here, and all of a sudden there is this wonderful golden day.

there are good days even during bleak times in our lives

The sky is that particular shade of blue that only hapens on days like that. The sun is warm and nurturing. There's a soft breeze

that rustles the leaves in the trees and
whispers through the grass in the meadow.
Everything smells nice.

**visual, auditory,
kinesthetic, and olfactory
imagery**

Over on one side of the meadow there's a
grove of trees—and as you look at that grove,
you wonder at how many shades of green there
are in nature: light green and dark green,
grey-green and blue-green, apple green, forest
green, olive green—and perhaps here and
there a flash of scarlet or gold.

**invitation to "see" the
familiar in a new way**

You wander over towards the grove, but
before you reach it you find, to your surprise,
that there is a small river between you and the
grove—a little brook. You hadn't seen it
because of the tall grass in the meadow.

You look around and, sure enough, you find
a little bridge or some stepping-stones or a
fallen log—some way to cross the brook; and
as you step onto the bank on the other side,
you sense that there is something different
about this other side of the brook—hard to
define, elusive yet somehow enticing, inviting
you to explore.

**symbolic of going from
a known place to an
unknown place**

You begin to wander through the grove. It
is so lovely. The sunlight filters through the
branches, making filigree patterns on the
path; small forest flowers peek out from
behind mossy tree trunks and sheltering
ferns, there are tiny reflecting pools, perhaps
a squirrel or chipmunk, the song of a bird.
There is a wonderful sense of serenity and
peacefulness.

suggestive of inner peace

You wander through there, soothed and
comforted and somehow strengthened by
that calm place.

After some time, you notice that the smooth path has changed a bit. It's a little narrower, and seems to have a slight slope upwards, and you think to yourself that it is probably time to go back; but for some reason you continue to follow the path.

first intimation that the peacefulness may change, but we tend to ignore it

And as you follow it, you notice soon that it is definitely changing—in fact, it has become quite steep. And the trees have somehow closed in so that the sky is shut out. And the further you go, the steeper that path—more of a trail, really—has become and the closer the trees until you realize with a little shock that you are in a dense forest, climbing up a very difficult trail and there is for some reason an insistence within you that you keep on going.

then we sometimes find ourselves in the thick of it without quite realizing how we got there, and/or have ignored the signs.

but we also know that somehow we must keep going

The trail gets steeper and more and more difficult. It is really more of a guess, now, where the trail actually is; the rocks are treacherous, you often slip and get muddy and scratched with the branches and brambly undergrowth, you skin your knee and twist your ankle as you climb over and crawl under fallen logs and you are *so tired*—and you think to yourself "This is crazy! Why am I doing this? I must go back!"

Yet still you continue.

After a long long time, the trail suddenly changes quite noticeably, within a few yards. It is easier to travel along, much less steep, the trees seem to have been left behind. But you are in the midst of a dense, dense fog, so that you have no idea whatsoever where you are or where you are going. And you say to yourself yet again, *"I must GO BACK!"* And you keep going forward.

The situation may ease, but we are still bewildered

You realize that, although the fog is so thick, you can see the edges of the trail and as long as you watch each footstep, you can stay on it. For some reason, this makes you feel safer. So you continue, and this part of the journey also takes a long time.

"watch your step"— especially when the situation is bewildering

And then — again quite suddenly — within a few yards the thick mist seems to evaporate away and you find that you are high up in the most beautiful alpine meadow. The sun is so brilliant, the sky that incredible blue. You look back and see that, yes, indeed, you were going through dense fog — in fact, it looks rather like a storm cloud. Through the lower part of the cloud you can see the tops of the trees in the forest and below that the grove of trees, and then the silver ribbon of the little river and the postage stamp of the meadow.

clarification

looking back, you can see how you got there

Then you turn, and look OUT — and you realize that you can see farther than you have been able to see, for as long as you remember — way, way out in the distance, right across the horizon.

And things look very different from up here. For instance, you see that there are many, many roads down there; and that they all lead somewhere! Some roads lead to certain places — towns, maybe — and some places have many roads leading to them, and some only a few; some roads lead to other roads and some lead back to the same road again, but they all lead SOMEWHERE. And somehow this makes a certain kind of sense that is hard to put into words but has meaning for you.

a different perspective

new patterns are emerging

So you look around and find a sunny rock to lean against, and you sit there for a long time, just absorbing those meanings, just looking out.

important to take time for reflecting

By and by, you realize that the sun is
beginning to dip in the west, and it really
IS time to go back now. But you also know
that you will be perfectly safe, that as long
as you put one foot ahead of the other
carefully, watching where you're going,
holding on to branches of the trees that
reach out for you, going carefully, you'll
be alright. You know that you will be
able to make the journey safely, because
you've already done it and you arrived
at your destination, even though you
wondered where the trail led to, and
it was so very difficult.

watch your step

**there may be friends who
reach out a helping hand**

**there are times when you
just have to keep going**

Now you know where you're going, and
that you will arrive safely.

we learn by experience

And so you travel back along that rough
trail, managing it slowly and carefully but
with assurance, back through the fog, down
the hazardous steep slope through the dense
forest, slipping and falling once or twice but
always able to catch yourself, until you find
yourself back in the lovely grove again, the
serenity and peacefulness once more
comforting you.

**the trail through life
is always hazardous in
places — with care it will
be negotiated safely**

Then, back across the little river, and into
the meadow.

FANTASY TRIP TO THE ROCK

*(I always begin this trip with the same "meadow"
introduction that I use in the trip to the top of
the mountain)*

. . . You hadn't seen it because of the tall grass
in the meadow.

Some day it might be fun to find out where that little river comes from but today, you're going to find out where it leads TO.

rivers can be followed in both directions

And so you begin to follow the path along the bank of the river. And you find that this little river changes many times as it pursues its lifestream. At times, it is a pastoral brook, the way it was when you first found it; at times, it broadens out, wide and shallow, the sun sparkling and dancing on its ripples, the water so clear that you can see every stone on the river bed.

our "life's stream" changes many times

metaphor for the various stages and experiences in our lives

Other times it is narrower, deeper, twisting and turning, with suggestions of little eddies and back currents that make you wonder about the forces beneath the surface.

there are always undercurrents and "forces beneath the surface"

And there is one stretch where the trees come so close to the river's edge that they blot out the sun, and the roots of the trees jut up through the path so that you have to watch carefully where you place each step, lest you should trip and fall. And it is dark and chilly along there, lonely and depressing; and it seems to go on for such a long time.

we all remember times when we had to "watch our steps"

there can be lonely times

But, in time, it does seem to be getting a bit lighter, and you look up and can see small patches of blue through the branches, and the trees begin to space apart, the sun filters through, and the patch becomes smooth once more.

The river now seems somehow to become more determined as it turns towards its destination. And sure enough, in a short time you come to the place where it meets a larger body of water — a lake or an inlet — it's hard to tell — and happily flows into it.

the "homestretch" seems to bring special energy

It's a lovely place. There's a little beach—there doesn't seem to be anybody there and yet it seems rather welcoming. Hear the gentle sound of the water against the shore; you may be able to hear the call of a bird or a loon, or the soft splash of a fish a few yards off shore. Perhaps you take off your shoes and socks so that you can feel the pebbles under your feet and the warm sand between your toes.

visual, auditory, and kinesthetic imagery

You wander along the beach in a happy sort of daydream and then, as you go around a curve, you find that the beach suddenly comes to an end. There's a huge outcropping of rock, and the beach becomes just a little strip at the foot of the rock.

whoops! was it too good to last?

With your shoes back on, you walk across this little strip, putting your hand against the rock to steady yourself so that you don't get your feet wet. And you immediately become aware of a rather strange feeling—as if there is some sort of strength coming into you, through your hand, from the rock.

strength from an unexpected source that at first seemed to be an obstacle

And as you get around to the other side, because of course this is a magic rock, there's a door into the rock and it's a little bit open, a little bit ajar.

invitation to find out more

You go in, and find yourself in a huge entrance hall, a sort of atrium. Once again, there doesn't seem to be anybody there but, once again, it seems like a welcoming place. It is a beautiful space. One of the first things you notice, over against one wall, is a huge bank of safety deposit boxes; and you somehow know that those are there for you to take off and deposit any worries, concerns, or burdens that you may be carrying, in any part of your life.

get rid of "excess baggage" before you explore, but put it in a *safe* place in case you need it again

So you do that, using as many boxes as you
need, locking them carefully and putting the
keys in a very safe place, perhaps on a ribbon
around your neck.

**important to know where
the keys are**

Feeling much freer now that you are relieved
of the weight of those burdens, you continue
to explore the entrance hall, and after a while
you find, in a little alcove, the opening to a
corridor.

**"excess baggage" can hold
you back in life**

And somehow you know several things.
You know that you are going to go down that
corridor, and that it will be perfectly safe,
but it will seem very strange; and all of those
things happen.

**this seems new but some
part of you knows about it**

You do go down the corridor, and it is
perfectly safe, but it certainly seems strange.
There's a sense of déjà vu, although you don't
remember being there before. It's warm, and
yet the air is fresh; it's dark, and yet somehow
you can see.

**important to assure the
person that he/she is safe**

And for some, the corridor is short, straight,
and for others, longer and perhaps more
twisting; for some, narrow, for others, wider,
but for everyone it leads eventually to the most
beautiful room you have ever seen. It is just
simply splendid! It seems as if it is filled with
sunlight — you know that that is impossible
yet that's how it seems.

**allows each person to create
his/her own corridor**

**visiting an "Inner Room"
can be enlightening**

Somewhere in that room you will find
somebody or something that has some
information for you — something to
communicate.

It may be a person and, if it is, you may
recognize him or her or you may wonder

whether you've ever met before; but it may not be a person. It may be a book or a letter or a photograph, something on radio or television, some memento from a cedar chest you may find there; it may even be a puppy or a kitten, or a toy. Somebody or something that has some information for you.

allows for any sort of communication imagery the person may have

communication can also come from childhood security symbols

And this information may come in words, or as a clear thought, but more likely it will come as a sort of feeling, an intuition: a clarification, perhaps — the good old *AHA!* response; or finding a link between some factor in some situation and some other factor in some entirely different situation, and understanding the link is helpful for you. Or it may just be a sense that somewhere, way deep in your inner self, something is shifting, some process is going on that will bring resolution in time.

information from the subconscious is seldom very specific — usually intuitive

Spend a litle time in that room now, as long as you like in hypnosis time and a minute or so by clock time, to fully enjoy that beautiful place.

dissociation suggestion regarding time

(Allow a minute or so of clock time)

That's right.

reassuring voice

It's time to leave that room for now. But you know, you can always come back here, any time you wish; because that room belongs to you. It is *within.*

reinforcement that thʳ "...information thʳ need..." is withʲ own experiencʳ

For now, come back up the corridor and into the entrance hall. And if you really must, you can retrieve one or some of the burdens that you have stored there. But you know, safety deposit boxes are SAFE.

why ʳ exc geι

And then out of the door, leaving it a little
bit open for when you wish to return; and
back around the small strip of beach at the
base of the rock, once again putting out your
hand to steady yourself and once again feeling
that strength, support, stability, security that
comes from *within*.

**opportunity for reinforce-
ment in own self-hypnosis**

**therefore, of course, from
within the person**

And then back along the beach, and
along the path by the river, and into the
meadow.

LEAVES ON THE POND

(This fantasy also takes place in a meadow)

As you go comfortably into hypnosis today,
take yourself to that beautiful golden meadow,
on a beautiful golden day, where you may
have visited before.

**reinforcement of previous
hypnotic experience**

Sense, with all your senses, the colors and
images and sounds and aromas that you find
there, and FEEL yourself there, in that
beautiful place.

utilizing *all* the senses

Over on one side of this meadow today, there
is a lovely little pond. In fact it is really just a
widening out of a small river as it winds its
way through the meadow, but the result is this
lovely little pond.

Beside the pond, on a grassy knoll, there is the
most wonderful tree. You will know, in your
own imagery, whether this tree has blossoms
on it, or leaves. I am going to describe it as
having leaves because that is the way it is in
MY imagination—but you know what YOUR
imagination sees.

personalizing

**permission to translate
into own imagery (some
subjects think it is "wrong"
to do that)**

You wander over, and sit down on the
grass beside the pond. It is crystal clear,
reflecting every light and shadow: the clear
blue of the sky, little skittering clouds, the
leaves on the tree (every leaf so clearly
defined), your own face.

Just as you are enjoying these lovely
reflections, a sudden gust of wind comes
along, and before you know it, the surface of
the pond has been covered with the leaves that
have been blown from the tree. All the reflections are gone — obscured by the leaves.

**"reflections" — multilevel
meanings**

**sometimes, there are
unexpected interferences
in our "reflections"**

You watch the leaves floating on the surface —
and in a few minutes you realize
that they are moving, gently propelled by the
little current in the river. Some of them just
seem to be swirling slowly, aimlessly about;
but some of them have begun to drift to the
edge of the pond, coming to rest under little
overhangs or in back eddies along the bank;
and some are drifting, gently but purposefully,
towards the end of the pond where it again
becomes a river — and these leaves soon drift
right out of sight.

**the interferences may not
make much sense at first,
then may begin to show a
pattern**

The leaves that have come close to the bank
settle into their safe little harbors; you could
touch them if you were to reach out.

It occurs to you that you could use those leaves
as little boats — tiny cargo boats, in fact. You
could put some small cargo on each leaf, and
let the current take it somewhere. And then
you realize that the "cargo" could be some little
worry or care that you have been carrying
around, some small burden. Or you could
perhaps put a heavier burden on several
leaves.

**implanting the therapeutic
suggestions**

**one part of you does not
have to bear the burden
by itself**

Explore those possibilities. Onto each leaf, place some small cargo — letting the leaves carry the burdens that you have been carrying. And so soon those cares, worries, concerns are also carried by the current — some drifting to the edge of the pond, where you could scoop them out again if you wanted to; some going on down the river, out of sight; and a few just swirling lazily on the surface until they, too, are carried downstream or to the bank of the pond.

there are many possibilities for dealing with the "burdens"

things on the surface may obscure the deeper issues temporarily

And soon you begin to realize something else. As the leaves, with their burdens, are moving with the current, so the surface of the pond begins to clear. And soon, once more, you begin to see the reflections of the sky, and the tree, and your own face.

as you clear away the burdens, you can begin to reflect clearly ("see things clearly") once more

(Make your own transition to any special message that is à propos for your patient, in or out of hypnosis.)

CORRIDOR METAPHOR

Sometimes, the subconscious continues to work hard at protecting us even though we have explained the need to make some changes. We feel that we are getting stuck, and we may wonder why.

the implication that the subconscious learned a necessary/appropriate response at some earlier time and continues to respond in that way gets away from guilt and self-blame

When that happens, it is often useful to use a metaphor — because metaphor is the language of the subconscious. I'm going to describe such a metaphor for you this morning; then you can adapt it to suit your own needs, in your own way.

"why use a metaphor?"

responsibility back to the subject

Imagine yourself at the beginning of a beautiful, long corridor — as if you are in a really elegant hotel. It is a lovely corridor, with beautiful lighting, with pieces of sculpture, with pictures

on the wall; there are plants; there is a
wonderful carpet. It is really a delightful
place to be. On either side, there are many
doors leading from this corridor. The doors
are closed, but can be opened from the
corridor side.

**therefore safe; to open
them is under the control
of the subject**

You are going to take a walk along that
corridor, on that lovely deep carpet, enjoying the sculpture, the paintings, the flowers,
the plants, and the effects of the lights;
perhaps there is a skylight sending down
a shaft of sunlight to bathe the corridor
in its golden glow.

**"sunlight" is a healing
image; "golden" is a
healing color**

From time to time, you may feel yourself
drawn to one door or another of the rooms as
you go by. When you feel yourself drawn to a
door, that is a signal to you, from you, that
that room needs to be entered because of
some unfinished business.

**"to you, from you" —
hypnotic language**

It may be something that is indeed finished,
and simply needs to be sealed or delivered or
formally completed. There may be something
that needs to be set free. There may be
something in that room that is wonderful to
visit again, to enjoy that experience all over
again, that memory, whatever it might be.

There may be something in that room that it
is time to deal with — something you have just
been putting to one side until the right time.

All kinds of possibilities — one room that
may have something wonderful to revisit and
one room with something that needs to be set
free and another room may have something
to be completed — that it is SAFE to be
completed — now.

**fear is the major reason for
procrastinating; now it is
*safe***

Make your way in your own time, down this
corridor. Take your time and then, when you
feel yourself drawn to any door, you can go
and visit that room.

One of the most interesting things about
this journey is this: you may feel a little
apprehensive about one room or some of the
rooms; but you can be very reassured that if
you are being drawn to that room, then it is
time to do something about it. If there are
areas that still need to be kept subconscious
then they WILL still be kept subconscious and
you will pass by that door, perhaps to visit it
on some other journey at some other time.

**safety factor and
permission to pass by**

So you can feel safe if you are drawn to a
room, because it *is* time for that room to be
explored or enjoyed again or be set free or be
worked on or be modified or whatever it might
need to be.

Take your time, take as long as you want in
hypnosis time and a couple of minutes by clock
time, just to visit those rooms. You can do that
in your own way.

**people in hypnosis accept
the concept of "hypnotic
time" vs "clock time" very
easily — this is an example
of trance logic**

When you are finished visiting any particular
room, go back into the corridor. You can
either leave the door open or you can close it
again, whichever seems appropriate to you.
Sometimes, if there is something in the room
that needs to be set free, you may leave the
door open and the windows as well so that it is
REALLY free. That might be something like
an old grievance, for instance, an old wound
that has healed over but the pain is still there
and it is time now for the pain to go; or an old
misunderstanding that can now be cleared up
and set free.

letting go

Some rooms may be won ˈerful fun to revisit—
it might be a particularly happy scene from
childhood or something that you shared with
a friend, something that is really lovely to
remember, so nice to remember that you can
almost feel yourself right there again, enjoying
all the feelings, all the emotions and responses
that were part of that event.

**invitation for pleasant
hypnotic regression**

If it is something that it is time to deal with,
you'll be surprised at how surprised you'll be
that you can deal with it so well. Somehow,
there will be a new approach come in to your
mind, a new way of looking at it that will just
be there for you. I wonder what it will be? You
can be very curious about those possibilities.

hypnotic language

So take your journey down that corridor, and
I'll be quiet for a little time while you do that.

**usually 2–3 minutes by the
clock; subjects appreciate
the silence**

Now, of course, you still have as long as you
need in hypnosis time and you have another
half-minute or so by clock time, so that you
can just gauge your own visiting—knowing,
too, that you can always come back to this
corridor and re-explore it, and you will probably
want to do that sometime in the future.

**there are further
opportunities**

When you have explored all the rooms that
you are going to explore at this time, let me
know about that by taking a big deep breath.
That's right.

**they usually take a deep
breath within one minute;
if not, I may take a deep
breath to "remind" them**

And how interesting it is that such a journey
can bring back to the conscious mind—things
that have been in your subconscious for such
a long time.

So you are back now in the main corridor and
you have visited the rooms that you are going

to visit this time. And as you come to the end of the corridor, you find that there is a T-junction, so that there is a branch going off to the left and one going to the right. I wonder which one you are going to choose? I do know that you are going to choose the one that is right for you at this time. This next corridor also is beautiful and has many rooms leading from it, and some day you may wish to come back and explore those — and the corridor is there for you whenever you wish to do that.

bridging to future work

At this time, though, that corridor will bring you, still comfortably in hypnosis, back to this room.

then the therapist can use his/her usual routine to end the hypnosis session

14

Memory and the Retrieval of Memories

There are various kinds of "memory":

1. "Being there"
2. Watching the situation on a TV or video screen, or in a movie
3. Watching from the outside
4. "As if being told"
5. "I just *know* what happened." This is knowledge vs. memory—one then finds ways to convert knowledge to memory
6. As if watching someone else—particularly for "scary memories"

There are also various ways of experiencing memory:

1. As if one were there—visually
    —kinesthetically
    —auditorially
2. As if watching—note that there may be an emotional component, as if one were watching a tear-jerker or a funny movie

One way to encourage memory is to ask the subject to think of something *around the time of* the event that they wish to remember more clearly. This time could be before or after the event. Then, the memory is gradually extended until all the edges are touched, then even more gradually until the subject spontaneously begins to remember quickly.

Often, at this stage, the memories begin to catapult over one another, so it may be useful to ask the subject to go over them again, *now that they have been retrieved,* so that they can be put "into their rightful place" in the conscious memory bank.

Remember (!) that memories retrieved in hypnosis may NOT follow through into the alert state, so you may wish to invite them to do so. Prepare the subject for this, saying that the conscious mind will remember when it is ready.

Once again I must make the disclaimer that we are not speaking here of horrendous memories of child abuse. Those memories are processed differently (see Goleman, 1992, in the Research and References section) and are often stored behind strong amnestic barriers until, through the course of long and difficult therapy, they can safely be allowed out.

We are talking about memories that may indeed be difficult or painful to retrieve, but are much more accessible both because of their content and the way they have been processed and stored by the wise subconscious mind.

And we are also talking about memories that a writer might want to rediscover for his/her work or personal enrichment, or that someone just wants to remember, some of those bygone days that have warm associations.

ENHANCING MEMORY

(The subject is in hypnosis)

You are very interested in enhancing your memory skills. You have told me that you USED to have a very good memory, but lately you seem to forget all kinds of things — some of them trivial, but some more important.

So we're going to consider a variety of ways to restore your memory. And the first thing is to know that YOU HAVE THE KNOWLEDGE THAT YOU SEEK.   **the memory and the knowledge are both there**

State that to yourself, several times. Yes, you do have that information. That's right.   **reinforcement**

One of the easiest ways to recover a little piece of information that seems to have gotten itself misplaced is to simply ask your subconscious to find it for you. "Subconscious," you can say to yourself, "I need to remember such-and-such. Please bring it back to mind before the   **(an extremely simple and very useful technique — that WORKS!)**

end of the day." Then, remember to thank yourself, when you suddenly remember it!

Another useful approach is to take some time out, go into hypnosis, and travel back to some related experience that you know you remember clearly, at about the same time in your life that you wish to recall.

Fill in all the details surrounding that time. Each detail contributes more information, fills in the picture more clearly. Go forward or backward in time, to the hours or days or weeks (whichever is applicable) before and after the remembrances that you seek. You may find it more useful to BE THERE, in your imagination, or to be watching from a distance or as if the scene were on a TV screen.

information triggers further information

for some, watching is more useful — possibly it is safer

As the details unfold, more details come to mind until you are remembering things that you thought were long-forgotten.

Some people with a great deal of experience in hypnosis can put themselves into a very special level of eyes-open trance and begin to write about what it is they want to remember, and as they write, they find they are writing about what they thought they had forgotten.

a type of automatic writing

Another variation on this theme is to think of the situation as a picture in a frame. There are blank places in the picture, as if some pieces were missing, or the artist hadn't finished yet. Ask the artist in you to complete the picture.

one need not be "an artist" to respond to this metaphor — but it can be adapted in any way *for* artists, or for musicians (fill in the missing notes), etc.

Tell yourself a story, describing the situation that you want to remember. Then ask your subconscious mind to help you tell it, by providing more details.

may remind the subject of his/her childhood

These are some suggestions as to possible
routes you may follow to retrieve information
that is too deeply stored at the present time.
Let us put some of this into practice now.

Settle yourself even more comfortably into
hypnosis. That's right.

And take yourself back to the time when you
were fourteen, to your fourteenth birthday.

Where did you live at that time?

*(Note: you may find that your subject spontaneously
answers these questions aloud. Respond briefly with
"Uhmmm" sounds; if he has been answering but
there is no answer forthcoming after a few seconds,
say softly in a very matter-of-fact voice, "That detail
will come into your awareness in its own time,"
and go on to the next question. But many people do
NOT answer aloud. Just give enough time between
questions for them to form their answers.)*

Think of your house, going through it room
by room — the front yard, the front door, the
back door, the kitchen, the living room, the
bedrooms — all of the rooms in your house.

**the house of one's
childhood is one of the
most emotionally evocative
of all memories**

Remember your school, where it was and what
it looks like from the outside; then your own
classroom. Who was your teacher *(or homeroom
teacher, or favorite teacher, etc.)?*

Think about your friends — your best friend,
the little gang you went around with. Were
they with you on your fourteenth birthday?

What did you do on that day? Did you go
somewhere? Did your friends come to your
house? Just let all sorts of details from your

filling in more details

memory bank come back into your awareness now. And you may be very surprised, and perhaps quite amused, at what pops into your mind. Just LET IT HAPPEN. I'll keep quiet for a few minutes, so that you can enjoy all that you are rediscovering.

delightful rediscoveries (if rediscovered, then obviously already there; further reinforcement)

(Stay silent for twenty or thirty seconds)

(Softly) That's very good — and very interesting for you.

You may wish to ask your subconscious to let these memories stay with you even after you have come out of hypnosis. You can be assured that your conscious mind will remember what it needs to remember, when it is ready. And indeed, further memories will come, because you will be thinking of these that you have rediscovered today many times in the next few days and that process will enhance the recovery of even more memories.

further invitation to the subconscious to allow the CONSCIOUS mind to remember

You have learned a great deal today about your own ways of remembering. You can use that knowledge in the future, adapting it to meet your needs, at any particular time.

you now have further information

15

Ego-Strengthening

Opportunities for enhancing self-esteem and finding positive inner strengths are always useful in any therapeutic plan.

The techniques decribed in this section are wider in scope than the simple (but very useful) "every day in every way, I'm getting better and better" type of statement. They are *invitations* to find one's *own* ego-strengths through imagery and metaphor, as well as in more substantial suggestions (e.g. "clarifying 'shoulds'").

Some people respond better to more direct suggestions, some to looser, more indirect suggestions. You will have a good idea of which to focus on through your evaluation of your client or patient. However, even for the most "directly bound" individual, I think it's only fair to at least OFFER a lateral approach, and you may therefore find these samples helpful.

I believe that it is extremely important to express appreciation of the self— literally, to "thank yourself for the good work that you are doing for yourself." A strong sense of self—ego-strength—is the core of confidence and self-esteem. Therefore, I will always put that suggestion into the opening phrases of the hypnotic interaction: "While you are settling into your own best level for this session, take a little time to say 'Thank you' to yourself for the good work that you are doing. You know that if someone else was doing such good work, you would be the first to commend and support them. Be as generous with yourself. . . ."

Egotism is, of course, the opposite of ego-strength and you may wish to discuss this with some of your patients if you sense there may be some confusion.

BRIDGING PAST AND FUTURE

Think of yourself in a lovely valley, with
gentle slopes of low hills on either side.

142

A bridge spans the valley. It is a beautiful bridge, just the kind you like best, and just exactly the right height for you to feel really comfortable when you are on it.

important for people to determine the height of the bridge themselves

Within the supports of the bridge, there is a stairway up to the bridge itself. Find those stairs, and climb up to the bridge, walking to the center of the span.

Now, turn and look back to the approach to the bridge, so that you can see where it has come from. Look at the road leading to the bridge, and the very, very harsh and difficult terrain that it has traversed on its way — so difficult that at times you wonder how you could have ever managed that journey — but you did. You did — and now you are on the bridge.

implication that the person has struggled very hard to achieve his present situation — through desperately difficult conditions

Look at that road leading to the bridge. It will show you how you came to this lovely valley. Look back, and *see how far you have come!*

Now look down, over this valley, which is the present. You will probably find that it looks a little different from this vantage point. You can see things that may have escaped your eye when you were right down among them — the familiar so often becomes unremarkable. You may notice some things that need attention — something around the homestead, a fence to be mended, a roof to be fixed, a garden to be weeded, a path to be cleared. Somehow, it is easier to see those things from up here. Take note of them in your mind so that you can attend to them when you go back down.

from a different perspective, everything looks different, and we can be aware of things that otherwise we gloss over or take for granted. Also a metaphor for repairing relationships, quarrels, personal problems of any sort

Turn now and look to where the bridge leads. This new road looks so interesting, and so much

more rewarding than the road you have left
behind — yet you can see that there are going
to be challenges along that road, too. But you
notice that even when the road disappears
behind a hill or into a valley, you can see it
reappear again later on; when it climbs a steep
mountain, it returns. You can see patches of
sunlight and patches of shadow, green fields
and forests, dry hills and flat prairie, rivers
and side roads.

there is a future, which looks more inviting because of past struggles; but the future also may have struggles

Look forward to this new part of your
journey — the road leading to where you will
be going past when you are ready to leave the
valley. And then, return to the stairway
leading down from the bridge, ready to mend
the fence, fix the roof, weed the garden, or
clear the path that needs your attention now.

past experiences will help in the future

attend to those things that you have identified, NOW

GATHERING STRENGTHS AND RESOURCES

At times, it is important for us to be aware of
our own talents and attributes. A person may
feel that his or her self-esteem is at a low ebb.
That person needs to recognize his or her own
worth as a person.

There are many ways to improve our feelings
about ourselves. Here are four basic steps that
we can take.

The "Hunter Quartet"

First, IDENTIFY STRENGTHS. Everyone
has some strengths in his/her life. Look at
yourself more objectively, but at the same time,
from within — using your own hypnosis — to
identify your own strengths: the things that
you do well; the achievements that you may
have had. Did you always come first in spelling?
That is an achievement — one of your strengths.

Are you the one whom everyone can count on? Do you always remember to take the paper plates to the picnic? Will you baby-sit at very short notice for a needy neighbour? Or are you a staunch friend through thick and thin? Perhaps, for you, these are new ways of looking at "strengths." But they are valid. Everything that we have done, throughout our lives, is important in shaping what we are. When we can recognize the good things — at whatever age they occurred — we are recognizing our own self-worth. So take a little reconnaisance trip through your life, and find your own strengths. They are an important part of your resource storehouse.

many people diminish their own importance; this is emotionally unhealthy

Secondly, ACKNOWLEDGE FRAILTIES. Just take a look at those areas where you know you could use some strengthening, and accept them for what they are. Acknowledging our frailties is very different from berating or demeaning ourselves because of them. It just gives one a chance to put things in perspective — "Yes, these are areas that I can work on, to strengthen and improve."

"frailties" are simply areas where we know we can improve — and knowing we can improve is a strength

Thirdly, REVIEW PAST SUCCESSES. In some ways, this overlaps Identifying Strengths, but the two may be quite different in many respects. Strengths, for instance, include skills that we have learned, awarenesses that we recognize about our own talents. Past Successes means just that — situations where you have been a winner! And they are valid at whatever time of your life they occurred. Give yourself the pleasure, now and several times over the next few days, of *reexperiencing* some of those past successes. Take yourself back to that time; see, hear, FEEL yourself there. Tune in especially to the feelings, and enjoy them yet again.

we also tend to dismiss the achievements of childhood, but they are extremely important

invitation to a pleasant regression

Fourthly, CLARIFY THE "SHOULDS."*
We have already talked about the "Shoulds"
in earlier sessions, so let me just remind you
that there are two types of "Shoulds"—those
that come from outside, and those that come
from inside.

Those that come from outside are very important
because they provide information and an
opportunity to review your thoughts, but they
belong to the people who bring them. Inner **awareness of one's *own***
Shoulds, those that come from your own deep **priorities**
inner knowledge of what is right for YOU,
must always be given attention and priority.
Whenever you hear yourself saying, "Yes, I
should . . .," be sure which type of "should" you
are expressing, and place it in its proper priority.

Following these four steps at regular intervals
will help you to understand yourself better and
improve your sense of self-worth.

CLARIFYING "SHOULDS"

Today I'm going to talk about a word—a
funny little word. It is one that we use often,
many times a day. The word is "SHOULD."

S-H-O-U-L-D.

Just think of how frequently we use that
word: "I should do this, I should do that," or
"I shouldn't do the other thing," "I must do
something else"—which is just another way of
saying "should." The reason it is such a funny
little word is because, when we say it, it seems
to imply that we have accepted some sort of
obligation—"Yes, I should . . ."—and yet, often,
right along with it, there is simultaneously a

---

*For a complete description of "CLARIFYING SHOULDS," see below.

little niggle of resentment or irritation or annoyance or aggravation. And that is interesting, that we are apparently accepting the obligation and at *the very same time* experiencing that little niggle of resentment.

When we study that word more closely, we find that in fact there are two kinds of "Shoulds": there are the Shoulds that come from outside, and there are the Shoulds that come from inside.

offering rationale for the dilemma

Outside Shoulds are very interesting and very important. They give us an opportunity to see something from a different point of view, they often give us more information, they frequently indicate a level of caring on the part of whoever says them, they certainly deserve respect and consideration: *but they belong to the person who brings them.*

acknowledging/validating reasons for earlier "yes, I should"

Inside Shoulds are very different. Inside Shoulds reflect the very depth of what we feel is appropriate for ourselves, those things that we know are right for us, those standards and values that you know are right for you as a person, from your own deepest inner knowledge of yourself.

validating the intuitive knowledge of self — and therefore ego-strengthening

It is when the Outside Shoulds and the Inside Shoulds conflict, that we get that little sense of unrest or aggravation or resentment or sometimes out-and-out anger.

Aha!

So, when you hear yourself saying, "I should," and you are also aware of that little niggle, that is information for you. It is your subconscious tapping you on the shoulder and saying, "Take another look at this because there is something here that is conflicting — an Outside Should is in some way conflicting with an Inside Should. Just take another look." When you do that,

offering a way out of the dilemma

it is easier to accept the conflicting emotion in hypnosis,

and especially when you do it in hypnosis, you will almost always discover what the conflict is.

Now, you may (and we often do!) come to the same decision or conclusion: "Yes, I should do this. There are valid reasons, that I can accept, which override the negatives that are interfering." But you will have come to the decision from a different perspective and therefore with a different kind of willingness. In that way, the Shoulds can become congruent and congenial and get along together, and you will feel more comfortable within yourself.

where the effects of social pressure are diluted

there _are_ situations that demand acceptance of an Outside Should, and the subject can be comfortably with such a decision

REHEARSE SUCCESS

Today you have a wonderful opportunity to add a new dimension to your preparations for (… …… …………).

Get very comfortably settled — that's right — and take yourself a little further into hypnosis so that you can fully enjoy this experience. You can let me know when you know that you have reached that best level, by nodding your head or taking a very deep breath.

(Wait for the signal)

Good.

Now begin to go forward and bring the future into the present, until you find yourself standing on the speakers' platform in front of the whole student body. You have an important address to give, and you are very well prepared. You have done all your research — just take a

(specify some situation: this text applies to a University student running for office on Students' Council. You will want to change your text accordingly!)

"let me know when you know" — deepening language

time distortion and manipulation

"well-prepared" in a

few moments to remember that excellent research that you have done—and you have written your paper carefully and checked it over. You KNOW that you have stated your facts clearly in your paper, and have said exactly what you want to say.

hypnotic suggestion for preparation; also research and statements about the paper

emphasizing and validating the situation

Feeling the self-confidence that comes with this careful preparation, you enjoy looking around the auditorium as people come in and find their seats. You might recognize and nod to one or two acquaintances. That's right.

ego-strengthening and reassurance

The meeting begins and you hear yourself being introduced. It is a good introduction, just the right length and giving the audience the pertinent aspects of your reason for being there. As you stand up and approach the podium, there is a polite applause.

involving various senses— auditory, kinesthetic

(watch your tenses through- out this script—keep consis- tently in the future *present*)

Your notes are in the right order. You have practiced in front of the mirror, and you know to keep your head up so that your voice will project well; you speak clearly, with good inflection.

referring again to prepara- tion in the "future past"

As you speak, you can sense that the audience is listening carefully and paying attention to the points you are making. It is a good feeling, to know that they are with you as you present your argument. You finish on a high note, making a strong final statement.

ego-strengthening state- ments presuming success

Excellent!! Congratulations—listen to the enthusiastic applause! You have done extremely well, and have been well received. Perhaps there are some questions from the audience, to which the chairman asks that you respond. Your answers are clear and concise.

attend to as many details as is reasonable

Enjoy your success for a litttle longer — that's
right — and then let the future return to its own
time as you bring yourself back to this room
and this present *(say the date)*. You will find that
the good feelings of your success stay with you,
and your subconscious mind knows the best
way to utilize this experience.

reorienting of time

**posthypnotic suggestion
made at a particularly re-
ceptive time — there is a
final relaxation of vigilance,
once the suggestion to "begin
returning" has been made**

AFFIRMATIONS

You have been learning many ways through
which you can bring about positive change
in your life.

YOU are the one who knows about these changes
and why they are the right ones for you.

**each person is his/her own
best authority**

Another tool to add to your store is the use
of *affirmations*.

An affirmation is a statement about the future,
made in the present tense, as if it had already
happened in the past.

the definition is important

Yes, that's right. A statement about the
FUTURE, made in the PRESENT, as if
it *had already happened* in the PAST!

"It feels wonderful, now that I have passed
my exams."

When we speak in this way to ourselves, the
subconscious hears us stating a fact that *is yet to
be,* and therefore it scurries around to find the
best routes to nudge us onto, so that that fact
becomes a fact.

**the reason why the
definition is the way it is**

Wonderful! And you can do this *so easily!*

A statement about the future, made in the
present, as if it had already happened in
the past.

Furthermore, you can recite your affirmations
when you are in hypnosis, or when you are in
the alert state. A good time is when you are   **able to utilize in many**
doing something very routine — cleaning your   **circumstances**
teeth, or peeling the potatoes, or perhaps
waiting for a bus (or ON the bus). It works
well to recite each affirmation five times at
any particular instance. You may wish to
recite several, in sequence. How many, will
depend on your own feeling about that —
give yourself some feedback when you are
arranging your protocol.

Such a simple thing to do — and such
wonderful results can come from doing it.

Take a few minutes now to arrange three or
four for yourself, to get you started. Remember,
it is important to keep to the definition: a statement about the *future,* made in the *present,* as if
it had *already happened in the past.* That's right.

And make your commitment to yourself to recite
your affirmations regularly and frequently.

You can be very curious about how your   **provoking curiosity**
subconscious is going to find the right
pathways to lead you to those goals. So often   ***how* it will work, presumes**
the goals are much closer than we realize.   **that it WILL work**

Say your affirmations to yourself once again,
now, before closing this session, and then
bring yourself up out of hypnosis in your
own way and your own time.

PRIORITIES

Sometimes, we find ourselves still following an old pathway that we have been on for a long time, and we wonder why we are still there. Is that pathway still useful for us? Is it taking us where we want to go? Or is it yesterday's pathway, that we are somehow still stuck on?

setting a metaphor

We tend to get trapped by our past priorities. To find out a little more about that, let's think about priorities in general, for a few minutes.

People have widely differing priorities. For some people, top priorities have to do with health — physical, emotional, and mental. For others, material things are important: a house, a job, financial security. Still others value relationships most highly — the family, friends. And there are those whose top priorities are on the more metaphysical plane — world peace, the environment, justice.

assuring that the subject's priorities are valid

All of these priorities are valid for the person who values them. However, there are a couple of interesting things about priorities.

Just imagine that you have a pencil and paper in your hand, and you are going to write down the first ten priorities in your life today, just as they occur to you. In fact, you may find it interesting to do that later on today, when you are home again.

opportunity to learn something new about your priorities

If you do it exactly as I have just said, and have written them down just as they occurred to you, you will be quite bemused by what your list looks like. There will be some items on it that appear, on reflection, to be trivial; the order — when you consider it logically —

the incongruity is acceptable

may be quite different from what it would have been if you had thought carefully about what you were writing down.

Nevertheless, this is the way the list has formed itself, and you can be assured that there is a reason for every item, and for the place of every item, on that list.

Let us presume that you then put the list away. Six months later, do the same thing, without referring in any way to the first list. Write down the first ten priorities, as they come into your conscious mind.

Then compare the two lists.

They will be different. Some items on the first list will be gone from the second (indeed, when you read through the earlier list six months later, you may be astonished at some of the items there) and others will have appeared. Some that were high on the first list may be much further down on the second, or vice versa.

aligning the experiences and comparing them

Is one list "right" and the other "wrong"? On the contrary, both are right. But they may be very different.

Our priorities change as life goes on. And it is appropriate that they should. WE change, as we learn and explore and grow in understanding. But we need to stand back and take a look, every so often, in order to avoid that trap that I mentioned earlier—the trap of getting stuck in our OLD priorities. Because if that happens, we become pulled in different directions, and find ourselves having trouble in making decisions, or in feeling confident in our roles as parent, employer or employee, teacher or student, friend.

making the point

Your priorities are an important statement —
to the world but more importantly, to yourself —
about who you are and why you are that way.
Enjoy giving yourself the opportunity of
reconsidering them from time to time, weed-
ing out any that have served their purpose,
nurturing any that are a bit too fragile for the
present demands that are being put upon
them, and feeling completely confident in   **ego-strengthening**
your own values.

PART VI

CHILDREN

General Approach

Specific Problems

16

General Approach

Some of the most rewarding of all hypnosis comes from working with children.

Their minds are so elastic, their imaginations so unfettered that they joyously go along with almost any hypnotic journey that you might suggest.

It is important, then, for us to suggest journeys that are valid and worthwhile — those that open up the child's mind to further exploration that he or she can do on their own.

Children are smart. They catch on quickly to what we are doing, and are usually way ahead of us, waiting for us to plod along to the end of the story. If we will just give them the opportunity, most times they can provide their own therapeutic suggestions.

It is essential that we respect the child's PRIVACY for these journeys. Children are not often offered the luxury of privacy — adults are always intruding, wanting to know what the child is thinking or doing. They are therefore VERY grateful, and after checking it out, and finding that you really mean it, will respond by working at their own "cures" even more assiduously.

For very young children, the use of stories and songs offers the most scope. You can make up verses for a song the child knows, with both of you singing, or tell a favorite story with a slightly different twist (or ask the CHILD to provide the twist). Stories with the child as the protagonist are always popular. For children coping with pain, such as a hospital procedure, just telling a favorite story *without* any unexpected twist works wonders. Children often engage in perfectly good trances with their eyes open and considerable physical movement.

There is a beautiful video, produced and directed by Leora Kuttner, Ph.D., called *NO FEARS, NO TEARS: Children with Cancer Coping with Pain*. It was made on a grant from the Canadian Cancer Society, at Childrens' Hospital in Vancouver, B.C. It exemplifies the way children use stories and other natural techniques, such as blowing bubbles, to relieve pain. See it if you can — especially if you work with children. It is available from the British Columbia Division of the Canadian Cancer Society, in Vancouver.

Rocking and stroking are kinesthetic inductions that very young children — even babes in arms — will respond to. The rhythm is just as important as the motion. I will often hold a very young child on my lap, or have my arm around him or her and sway in rhythm. I feel very comfortable doing this but others may not, especially non-physicians. Be very attentive to minimal signals of uneasiness in the child.

And children can teach US — if we will allow them — how to remember being children ourselves, exploring the universe in a long-forgotten way. It is a special privilege to work with children.

OVER THE RAINBOW — A CHILD LIKE YOU

Today let's go on a magic carpet ride.
Just close your eyes and go to your own
magic carpet landing pad. Let me know
when you get there. *(Child will nod, or tell
you)* Good.

Now climb aboard that magic carpet, that's
right, and let it begin to lift off — ohh, *that's*
right — way off into the blue sky, way up above
the tree tops. What can you see from up there,
safe on your own magic carpet? Can you see   **allowing the child his/her**
all kinds of wonderful things? *(Child nods)*   **own imagery — a magic**
I'll bet it's just beautiful.   **carpet gives lots of scope**

Look! 'Way over there — see the rainbow?
Let's go on the magic carpet over to the
rainbow. That's right — right over to that
lovely rainbow. Find your own own special
color — the one you like the very best. Is it   **children are often**
green, or pink? *(Child may answer or not — if*   **fascinated with color**
not, just go on speaking after waiting a moment)   **and light**
Find that most special color and let your
magic carpet take you right into the very
center of that wonderful color. How
wonderful! Colors are so special.

Now, *keep on flying on your magic carpet RIGHT THROUGH the rainbow* to the other side! There you are on *the other side of the rainbow!* Very, very few people know what it's like on the other side of the rainbow — you're one of the lucky ones.

Wow! THROUGH the rainbow!

makes the journey very special

Let your magic carpet find a good place to land, and feel yourself settling down. That's right. Then do whatever you need to do to keep your carpet safe. Some carpets need to be tied down, while others just know to stay where they're put. Then climb down from your carpet so that you can explore that interesting place.

Look around you as you walk along. In a few minutes, I think you are going to meet — yes, there (s)he comes — a little boy *(girl)*. Do the you know, it's the nicest thing! — that little boy *looks just like you!* Isn't that amazing! *(Describe the clothes the child is wearing that day, and something about the child — hair color, etc.)* Yes, he looks remarkably like you.

easy way to establish the metaphor

That little boy has a problem, very very much like the one you used to have. *(State the problem very simply — pulling out eyelashes, wetting the bed, or whatever it is)* So he knows that YOU understand all about that. In fact, you are the ONLY one who really understands about that. So he knows that he can trust you.

"used to have" — implies successful change

emphasizing the child's awareness

In your own way, teach that boy what he needs to know so that HE can be finished with that problem, too. But do that just between the two of you — don't tell me about it! That's right — it's personal, just between the two of you. You can nod when you've told him what he needs to know.

offering the chance to teach himself what he needs to know

(Child nods) Good. Does he really understand?
(Another nod) Good.

But I think he has a couple of questions. For
instance, he might want to ask, "Does it really
work?" *(Leave a few moments of silence between
questions)* Will it work for me as well as you?
How do you know? And probably there are
one or two other questions that I don't know
about, too.

**the child will have
questions that he has
probably not asked you
nor anyone else — now
he can ask himself**

Yes, I thought so. You take as long as you
need, and when you've taken care of ALL
the questions, let me know.

(Child lets you know) Excellent.

Now it's nearly time to say goodbye to your
new friend for now. Probably, you will want to
come back and visit with him some other time.
You two can make your own arrangements.
That's right.

**there will be further
communication whenever
needed**

And now, time to go back to your magic
carpet. There it is. Climb back on, and take
off — there you are, coming back through the
rainbow — as beautiful as ever! — and over the
clouds, then down past the treetops to your
very one landing pad.

And when you've arrived safely, it will be time
to open your eyes. And here you are back in
this room! Welcome back.

17

Specific Problems

ENURESIS (YOUNGER CHILD)

(Note: I am very reluctant to treat enuresis in any child under the age of eight years; if I have made exceptions to this rule — possible, but not likely — I cannot bring them to mind. Before the age of eight, physical maturation may not be sufficiently advanced to provide success. In that case, we would hand the child another failure — surely not what we want to do. Up to the age of eight, then, treat the mother's anxiety and leave the child in peace.)

You like to watch television with your eyes closed when you come here, don't you? Umhum. Then close your eyes now, and turn on the television set. Is it on? No? — Oh, there it comes, good. Is it on the right channel? Find the one you want. That's right. What program are you going to watch today? *(Child will tell you)*

very simple way that children like to go into hypnosis

Ah, yes. You have a favorite character on that program, don't you? Who is that? Yes, a very special person *(animal, or however it is best described)* indeed.

favorite character has more impact

Just enjoy watching the program. Then, when it's over, you're going to have a wonderful surprise, because *(whoever that favorite character is)* is going to come and talk to you! Yes, to YOU yourself! You can tell me when you see *(him)* coming.

invoking child's curiosity

Is he coming now? Wonderful! And I think
that he has some very special things to tell
you — but very privately, of course, just
between you and him — some very special
things to tell you about something you want   **respecting child's privacy**
to understand better, or maybe something
you want to learn how to do, or learn how
to stop doing. You know what that is, don't
you? *(Child nods)*   **establishing the project**

Yes, I knew you did.

You and he can begin to have your visit, then.
I'll just keep quiet for a while. When he has
told you all about the things you need to
know, you can tell me that he's finished.

*(Sit quietly. Within a few minutes, child will tell
you, or nod.)*

Have you had a good visit? That's wonderful.
And he was able to tell you some interesting
things, so that you know what to do now?
Good. Are you going to start doing those
things tonight? *Very* good. Mummy will be   **suggestion linking project**
very surprised, won't she?   **to nighttime, i.e., bed**

(Child nods, happily)   **children love to surprise
                                                       Mummy**

Well, I guess it's time to turn off the television
set. Is it off? Good, then you know it's time to
open your eyes.

*(A variation on this theme, for the slightly older
child, is to have the TV personality meet the child
as in the earlier script, then the two of them go off
together on a journey)*

So the two of you ride off on your bicycles,
along that interesting trail. And do you know

what? That trail leads you to the desert! Do
you know what a desert is? Yes, that's right,
a very, very dry sandy place.

You ride out into the desert together, and soon
you find an oasis—a little group of palm trees,   **pleasant scene**
making a nice shady area, where there's a
lovely pool of water. So you get off your bikes
and sit under the palm trees and talk about—   **personal visit**
oh, about all *kinds* of things. *You'll* know what
you talk about.

Nighttime comes, and you eat some sand-
wiches that you find in your pack. Then you
both lie down on that wonderful warm, dry
sand, with the stars twinkling overhead,
and go to sleep.

And in the morning, when you wake up, you
are still there on that nice warm DRY, DRY   **the implication is obvious!**
sand, in the desert. You have a drink of water
(because your friend knows that the water is
safe). Then it's time to go home, and you get
back on your bicycles again and ride back to
the trail, and along the trail to your house,
where he has to say goodbye to you for now.

But you've had a wonderful visit, and you
know you'll always remember that special   **reinforcement**
night in the desert, sleeping and waking up
on the warm dry sand.

ENURESIS (OLDER CHILD)

Now you remember, of course, the last time
you were here we talked about ways that your
body can stay nice and dry all night, so that
you wake up in the morning in that lovely dry
bed—the same way that you did throughout

Friday night, and of course you know now that your body can do that, 'cause you've *done* it. That is one of the best things about it; when you've woken up to a nice dry bed, then you know that your body knows how to do that because it has done it.

child had reported a dry bed on Saturday morning

So there are a couple of interesting things about it, and the first thing that is kind of interesting is that you wonder why sometimes your body does it and sometimes not. So we are going to talk about that, first of all.

trance logic (which is also true!) and the simple assumption of success — children accept that very easily

curiosity invoked

Take yourself back to Saturday morning, waking up to that lovely, dry, warm bed and feeling so happy about that — just take yourself back two mornings ago when you woke up and Ohh! — that is such a delicious feeling, that wonderful dry bed, can't you just *feel* that — oh yes, a *wonderful* feeling, that's right.

regression to happy event

kinesthetic

Okay. Now, you know the deep part of your mind, the part of your mind that is much deeper than the thinking mind, has a far better memory even than the thinking mind does and that is the part of your mind that can talk to your body; they can communicate back and forth.

invoking the subconscious

mind/body communication

So I'm going to ask that part of your mind, that very deep part, and your body to go back while you are remembering how good it was to wake up like that in the morning, asking your body and your mind to go back through the whole night in memory, in the subconscious memory, and to find out about those things that happened, which were all the right things. Whatever happened that night *all the right things happened,* all the right combinations came together properly; so it is very useful for your body and that very deep part of your mind to

communication to "keep the good things happening"

find out exactly what happened that night,
because that was a successful night for you.

It proves to you that you know how to do it! **again!**

And so, what we are interested in now is
finding out what is different between the times
that you do it and the times that you don't do
it. Just remember that wonderful, wonderful, **kinesthetic**
wonderful warm dry feeling while your subcon-
scious mind, that deep part of your mind, and **subconscious review of**
your body go back through the whole night to **events that occurred while**
find out exactly what happened while you were **sleeping**
asleep, exactly what happened while you were
asleep, going back through the whole night **"re-viewing"**
minute by minute right through the whole
night and probably through a couple of hours
and even longer, before you went to bed — find
out what happened then, also. That's right.

And then, when that deep part of your mind and
your body together have remembered at that
different level of remembering, right back through
the whole night and a couple of hours before,
then they can start remembering in a forward
direction again. It's interesting how we can re- **hypnotic language**
member backwards and forwards; we can start
remembering in a forward direction again, **go over it again and again**
remembering forward through the whole night **for reinforcement**
with everything happening just the way it should,
so you can wake up in the morning warm and
dry and cozy and feeling so good about that.

And tonight, when you are doing your hypnosis **reminder to do self-hypnosis**
before you go to sleep, ask that deep part of your
mind to do the same things, to remember what
Friday night, right through the night to Saturday
morning, was like — first of all going backwards, **further reinforcement,**
starting when you wake up and then going for- **with kinesthetic imagery**
wards — that's the idea — and that feels so good.

Now, you remember that the last time we were talking about two different ways that that can be accomplished. The first way is for your body to give your mind a signal that you need to wake up to go to the bathroom; and because you are such a wonderful sleeper (you know what a good sleeper you are, don't you? — you are a wonderful sleeper, just the best sleeper in the whole world) so you sleep so well that your body has to be particularly good at sending messages because it needs to send a message that your mind hears and understands, *even when it is asleep!* — and that is a very special kind of understanding.

assumption of mind/body communication

ego-strengthening

trance logic

So you can ask your body to learn how to do that even better than it knows already (because it knows a lot already), to go and give your mind that message — yes, even when you're asleep, a good strong message to wake you up just enough to get up to go to the bathroom. You hardly even need to wake up at all, just enough to go to the bathroom, do what you need to do there, empty your bladder, go back to bed, still kind of dozy and then of course go right back to sleep again and finish your night's sleep and wake up warm and dry and cozy in the morning. That's one way.

good strong suggestion!

rehearse success

The other way — remember, we talked about it last time — was for your bladder to be able to stretch just a wee little bit more, the same way you can blow a little bit more air into a balloon and it will still be okay; because now your body is old enough to know how to do that, too. We are all different. And some people learn to do that earlier, some people learn to do it a little later, but everybody learns to do it after a while. Your body knows enough now to be able to do that, and you know that it does because from time to time it already does.

body imagery

ego-strengthening

repeat of earlier suggestion

So ask your body to learn how to do that even better than it already knows, just to be able to stretch that little extra bit, so that it can be comfortable and then when you wake up in the morning nice and dry and cozy and comfortable, you can get up and go to the bathroom and empty your bladder. And you may even want to go back to bed after that for a little while, if there is time before school, because it is so warm and dry and comfortable. That's right.

kinesthetic

And the best thing about all of that, is that you know that you know how to do it because you have already done it, in fact you already did it two nights ago. So, once again just remember that wonderful feeling of waking up sooo nice and dry and cozy and comfortable, and when you do that, of course, you can think to yourself, "Ohh, that is just super, my body is learning more and more about how to do that." And when you go to bed, you can think to yourself, maybe even the last thought before you go to sleep, "MY body knows how to do that! It will do all the right things: either it will send a message that is such a good strong message that it will get through even when I'm asleep or it will just do that little extra bit of stretching in my bladder so that I can wake up the next morning still nice and dry."

re-viewing again

ego-strengthening

And soon, EVERY night will be a nice dry night and you will wake up nice and warm and dry and cozy, every morning.

kinesthetic — appealing to child's sense of comfort and security

LEARNING DISABILITIES

(This is one of a variety of approaches to assist the learning-disabled child, bearing in mind that we are referring to types of dyslexia rather than to diminished mental capability.)

Just close your eyes, then, and take yourself
into hypnosis in your own way. How are you
going to do that today? *(Youngster answers)*
Good. You just go ahead with that, and enjoy
wherever your imagination takes you.

That's right. And then begin to include in
your imagination a HUGE train station. Just
the HUGEST train station you can possibly
imagine — maybe one of those immense train
stations in London or in Paris.

**(if the youngster has no
experience of train stations,
use an airplane terminal,
with planes landing on
runways from all directions,
taxiing to the special
arrival bay for each plane)**

There are dozens and dozens of tracks coming into this station. They're coming from
all directions — north, south, east, and west —
and they all have to somehow find their way
into the main terminal and then to one very
specific platform — the only platform that is
now waiting for that particular train.

So the trains come from all parts of the
country; then, when they are getting near
the station, they have to switch onto the tracks
leading to that one station (because there may
be several train stations in a very large city);
THEN they have to find the right set of tracks
to lead them to their *specific* platforms where
they are expected. Perhaps there are people
there waiting to board the train, or to meet
someone who is coming in; or maybe there
is freight to be off-loaded onto a waiting truck.

setting the metaphor

So it is vitally important that the train find
THE RIGHT TRACK to lead it to its own
particular destination.

When we are learning something, it is a little
bit like that. The information may come in
from all over the place — through our eyes
when we see, or when we read, or through

**relating the metaphor
to the experience**

our ears when we hear, or by means of other
sensations such as touch — to learn that
something is hot, for example.

Then, once the information gets into our
brains, it has to find THE RIGHT TRACK
to take it to the place where other, similar
information is waiting for it, so that the new
information can join that older information.

For instance, if we are learning something
in math, we want the new information to get
on to the right track to take it to wherever the
OTHER information about math, that we
already have, is waiting. Or, if we are learning
French vocabulary, we want the new words to
join in with the words we already know.

You can think of lots of similar examples.

**challenge the child to make
the technique "his own"**

So when you are getting ready to learn
something new — if you are settling down
to study at home, or just before you go to
school in the morning — take a few minutes
to go into hypnosis in your own way, then
begin to think of that train station; and ask
your deep, deep inner mind to put all that
new information that you are learning, onto
THE RIGHT TRACKS so that it will join
up with the knowledge you already have on
that subject.

**how to adapt the technique
to his needs**

And you will be amazed at how things come
together for you when you do that. Because of
course, *your* brain understands all about train
stations and how important it is to make really
sure that everything goes in the right direction.

*(Bring the youngster out of hypnosis in his or her
usual way.)*

FEARS AND NIGHT TERRORS

(This script is reproduced as verbatim as I can remember it from a session I enjoyed with a little girl in my own family practice. She was three years old at the time. She is sitting on the special examining table I have in the children's room and I have my arms around her, rocking her gently. We have been singing a little song, her eyes are closed and she is very comfortable.)

Mummy says that you sometimes wake up in the middle of the night, and you seem to be very very frightened. *(She nods)*	**bringing her attention to the problem**
So we'd better do something about that, hummm? So you can sleep comfortably the whole night through? *(She nods again)*	**presuming success**
Good. And of course you know that YOU can do something about it, don't you? *(Another nod, very sure)*	*child* **has the capability**
Yes, I know that, too. What are you going to do?	**getting the child to decide on the method makes success even more likely**
"Build a HIIGGHHH wall!"	
Wonderful! What are you going to build it out of?	**creating the image**
"Plasticine."	
The very thing! Why didn't I think of that? Are you going to *start right now? (Nods)* Good. Then I'll keep quiet for a little while until it's done.	**"start right now" is the suggestion**
(In a few moments, she nods again)	
Excellent. Is it all the way you want it? *(I sense a little unease)* I'll bet I know what's missing. Does it need a door?	**too much like a prison if no door**

(A fast nod, then again a little hesitation.)

BUT this has to be a *very special* door, doesn't it? One that can be opened ONLY BY YOU FROM THE INSIDE!! *OR* by Mummy or Daddy using a special magic key.

(A small sigh, followed by an emphatic nod.)

Of course. So you make your special door; and even, if you want to, a special window where you can see out but nobody can see in from the outside except, of course, Mummy or Daddy.

if there is a single parent, omit the inappropriate word; and unfortunately, in this day and age, we must always be mindful of child abuse — be particularly sensitive to any slight hesitancy

(A little frown; obviously this is hard work.)

"Okay, I'm done."

Wonderful. Will you show me around that very safe place that you have made? *(She nods)* Okay, you take me in — because, of course, that is the only way anybody or anything except you or Mummy or Daddy can get in, right? *(Another emphatic nod)*

this is the child's domain; I am the guest

Ohhh, isn't this nice! What a safe, cozy place! You have done a wonderful job. Thank you so much for showing me around. Shall we leave now? *(Nods and spontaneously opens her eyes, giving me a huge smile.)*

safety reassured

ASTHMA IN CHILDREN

Using hypnosis to help children with asthma relieve their symptoms is one of the most rewarding applications of this extremely adaptable modality.

In an excellent study, Dr. Olga Ferreiro (1986, 1993) demonstrated the efficacy of these techniques. So clear were her results that she was able to differentiate by their response to hypnosis between children whose asthma was triggered by infection, by allergy, or by emotion. Those whose attacks were sparked by emotion achieved the best and most rapid response; by allergy, the second best; by infection, a definite third. Of 50 children, only three did not respond and all of these had trouble within the home.

There was another interesting thing about this study: the pulmonary function tests showed marked improvement after hypnosis. This is not so with adults, who may get great symptomatic relief but do not show objective changes in pulmonary function.

The technique with children is simplicity itself: I ask them to show me how they have an asthma attack.

Children are spectacularly good at this approach — which would not work at all with adults, who would immediately want to analyze it and quite possibly refuse to subject themselves to it.

Case History

S.J. was a lad of 11 years. He had severe asthma and was on high doses of medication when he came into my practice. He was so dependent on his medication that he would not go to a school picnic, nor spend the night with friends for fear of "running out" of his medicine.

One evening I was to give a lecture on hypnosis to a group of colleagues. I asked S. whether (with his parents' permission) he would like to come and be a demonstration subject for me. He was excited at the thought. I had done no hypnotic work with him whatsoever before we went to the meeting.

At the meeting he sat quietly, waiting for me to call on him. He was very interested in what I was saying. When I asked him to come up, he did so with alacrity. I simply asked him to close his eyes and show us what happened when he had an asthma attack. Within moments, we could hear the rhonchi across the room — no stethoscope required!

Keeping a watch on him out of the corner of my eye, I explained about the use of hypnosis to the group. S. continued to wheeze markedly. Then I heard him say, "I-don't--like this-any--more!" — gasping and wheezing between each word.

I turned to him. "Oh, I'm sorry, S.!" I said. "You can get back to breathing normally now, if you like." Again, within less than 15 seconds, the wheezing subsided, the labored breathing eased, he quietened.

I turned back to continue my spiel to the group, again watching him out of the corner of my eye. He was deep in thought. After I finished speaking, he said to me, "That means that I can do it myself, doesn't it?"

S. went on to "do it himself" very well. In three months he had cut his medication in half and was able to go on school outings. By the end of a year he was just on a low maintenance dose of a single medication. By the time he was into his teens, he was free — of the asthma, the medication, and the fear.

Almost all children can learn to control their asthma attacks this way. The concept intrigues, rather than scares, them. It is wonderful for a child to realize that s/he has such mastery over something that has plagued him or her for so long.

PART VII

HABIT DISORDERS

Weight Program
Smokers' Program

18

Weight Program

Over the years, the Weight Program that we have offered in the office has steadily evolved; now, it extends for 12 weeks and involves myself, the psychologist who works in my office, and a nutritionist.

In the 12 weeks, there are weekly 1½-hour group sessions, and weekly 1:1 private sessions with one of the three of us—whoever is leading the group sessions at that particular time.

The three of us who lead the program agree on the basic principles: that obesity—especially long-standing, gross obesity where the individual has 50 or more pounds of excess weight—has nothing whatsoever to do with "willpower," quite a lot to do with metabolism, and a tremendous amount to do with self-image and self-esteem.

Accordingly, there are some ground rules in the group, and one of these is that the word "diet" is never used. DIET is a very bad word. It is totally punitive: it implies that one must suffer through a deprivation period until the diet is over and then one can get back to eating "normally"—which is why the person got to where he/she is, in the first place. Who could ever do well with a premise like that?

It is also a known fact that diets promote eventual weight GAIN rather than permanent weight loss, and this is particularly true for people who have the aforementioned long-standing problem.

Another no-no is that most sabotaging word in the English language—TRY.

It is so sabotaging because it is overtly positive, yet it always carries with it the possibility of failure. There are many things one can do, rather than "try." One can search, learn, explore, discover, find out more about—or just DO it, and all of these carry a much more positive connotation than "try." Just say, aloud, "I'll try that," versus "I'll explore that," and you will immediately confirm the concept for yourself. Whenever someone in the group says she (we have had very few men taking the group, although they are welcome) is going to "try" something, we will catch her up on it and ask her, firmly, "Would you please rephrase that?" Very quickly, the group members are monitoring each other and it becomes a game — a game with an important purpose. It encourages positive, rather than negative or (which is, perhaps, even worse) ambivalent self-talk. Positive self-talk enhances self-esteem.

We have divided the group sessions so that I give five, the psychologist gives five, and the nutritionist, two. My five are:

Reward Systems
Sabotage and Saboteurs
Metabolic Change, Mind-Body Communication, and
      State-Dependent Learning
Body Image; Self-Hypnosis
Battle Plans for the Future

Psychologist:

Self-Esteem
Assertiveness
Relationships
Stress Management
Behavior Modification

Nutritionist:

Food Management
Fitness

Every group session ends with a relaxation or hypnosis experience.

I usually take the first three sessions. The first week we talk about Reward Systems, especially the subconscious rewards. The conscious ones are much easier to deal with — and often they are difficult enough! Many of the subconscious rewards come from early conditioning, especially from childhood: eat up your dinner — good girl; don't leave food on your plate, think of the starving children in India; you must eat, or you'll get sick; don't cry — here's a cookie; good girl/ boy — here's a candy. (This will lead into the discussion of State Dependent Learning at a later session.)

The child receives the approval of the adult for doing what he/she is told, and that approval is the reward. It is a very, very powerful reward, indeed, to receive the approval of a parent or some other very significant person in the child's life. The homework (given during the group hypnosis) is for the subconscious mind to gather more information about the person's reward systems and to bring that up to more conscious awareness.

In the second session, we look at sabotage and saboteurs—especially the "Beloved Saboteurs" in the person's life. As soon as I say "Beloved Saboteurs," little nods of recognition ripple through the group. These are the very important people in our lives—mothers, spouses, sometimes children, teachers, the boss, a friend. They all seem to be acting with good intention, and indeed they would say so themselves, I am sure; but the result can be, and often is, devastating.

It is *because* they are so important that their influence is so great and carries *so much WEIGHT!* Dealing with a Beloved Saboteur is very difficult. How do you confront your mother and tell her not to bake you any more birthday cakes, when this is one of the ways she has been showing you that she loves you, for 40 years? We practice, role-play, write out the scripts, offer each other suggestions; I usually play Devil's Advocate and take the role of the saboteur. We discuss the importance of "I-messages": "Honey, I'm having a hard time with this program right now. Could you help me by not.......? I know you do that because you care for me, but for some reason I find it difficult. I know how much you want to help me and your moral support means more than I can possibly say."

During this session I also talk about PATTERNS, because there almost always are some, and realizing what the patterns *are* can be very illuminating. One technique is to pass out paper with the alphabet down one side of the page; each person in the group is to fill in words beside each letter that describe some sort of sabotage for them, e.g., Anxiety, Aunt Matilda, Anger; Birthday; Charlie, Cheesecake; Desk; Evenings, Emotions; Fatigue, Food, Frustration, etc. It is fascinating to see the patterns that are revealed in this simple exercise. One person will have a list full of people's names; another, emotional situations; a third, social scenes. Sabotage may be found in situations as well as in people. Recognizing the type of situation that is likely to be sabotaging is the first step towards changing: one can avoid the situation, or change one's involvement in it.

Homework is to practice confronting sabotage, in front of a mirror.

During this session, awareness of the Inner Saboteur also becomes clearer.

The session on changing metabolism, understanding your body, and mind/body communication is quite exciting. The group members are always fascinated to hear about the new developments in the realm of psychoneuroimmunology, psychobiology, and other such esoteric fields, and are delighted to hear that this information is relevant to THEM. We also discuss the concept of State-Dependent Learning more fully.

This may also be the session when I teach them self-hypnosis. Then they are to go home and practice what I have been preaching.

During the next three sessions, the psychologist takes the group through the world of assertiveness training, self-esteem, and managing relationships. Relationships change, sometimes drastically, for people during these projects. The sad truth is that in our society people treat you differently when you're thin than they do when you're fat. This is an insult to many people. "I lost 40 pounds and everyone told me how wonderful I was. Then I gained it back, and they suddenly all avoid me. But I'm the same person — just as good or bad, just as intelligent or not, and just as sensitive." Fat people tend to get overlooked at promotion time, or even passed over for the job to begin with.

And the relationship with family members can also be put to a terrific strain, particularly if sabotage has to be dealt with. (When one person makes waves, another gets splashed in the face.)

Self-esteem is the single most important issue. The group are gently led to identify their deep feelings and insecurities, to listen to their own deprecating self-talk (the Inner Saboteur), to recognize how very often they put themselves last on the list. Changing these patterns of behavior and interaction that they have been following for decades is a terrific struggle and one that we all can admire.

The homework for these sessions usually has to do with using their own self-hypnosis to rehearse change and to understand themselves better.

The nutritionist takes the next two meetings. She talks about food plans (NEVER "DIETS"); the newest information on cholesterol, high fiber, and complex carbohydrates; and an update on the latest knowledge about obesity, appetite "control centers" in the brain, brown vs. yellow fat. She also fields a thousand questions, which usually come straight from the latest women's magazines.

Each person in the group has an *individual* exercise regime arranged for her. For someone who has been sedentary for 20 years, and has also gained 75 pounds, a realistic exercise program will probably start with walking one block at a good pace and walking home somewhat more slowly. Swimming is a very good exercise for obese people and doing "swimnastics" is fun and very useful. Exercising in the pool is particularly good for those with arthritis.

During the next two sessions, the psychologist continues with stress management and behavior modification. By now, the group is coming to terms with the fact that this is NOT a dietary program, the pounds are NOT dropping off like magic, and *we* are not taking responsibility for *their* changes. Morale is often at a low ebb.

We know that this stage simply has to to be "got through." We encourage, encourage, encourage. "You will make changes when the reasons for changing are more important than the reasons for keeping on with the old ways." "Recognize your own worth." "Yes, you CAN." Slowly, things begin to improve and as they feel better about themselves — the pounds DO begin to drop off! Not spectacularly, but slowly and steadily their bodies begin to respond to the positive suggestions, improved self-image, and increased awareness of their own potential. They are resuming control.

By the time I get back to them, in the second-to-last session, the change in the dynamics of the group, personally and with each other, is almost palpable. I deal with body image, stressing that each one of them has a *wonderful* body; it has a heart that beats 70 times a minute, lungs that confidently keep breathing, brain cells that compute and emote, legs that have carried them around for years and years and years. Appreciate that wonderful body! Talk to it lovingly.

I do not believe that "inside every fat person, there is a thin one waiting to get out." In my experience, most of them cannot even imagine what it would be like to be thin and it is a frightening prospect — which is another reason why "diet centers" don't work. When pounds drop off with the diet, the inner self says "WHOA!" and scurries around to get back to "normal" again.

Remember that all habits begin for a purpose, I tell them. For some reason, years ago, your body (and your subconscous) came to the conclusion that adding on extra pounds was a very important thing to do. Because that inner self believed that so implicitly, for so long, it has been diligently doing its best to maintain that status ever since. The thing to do is to *respect* that and say to yourself, "Thank you for the INTENTION; I understand that you believed I needed to do this/be like this for some important purpose. But whatever that reason or that purpose was, it is now finished, obsolete. Please help me put it finally away, and get on with a new pattern for the present and the future."

On the last evening, we discuss "Battle Plans for the Future." What are you going to do, *instead* of reaching for food, in those situations that you have identified? It is very important to include this topic in any such program, so that they can prepare and feel that they are still in control of the situation.

There are some issues that come up time and time again in the groups. Issues surrounding sexuality are common; marital problems — everything from the autocratic spouse to infidelity; grappling with overprotective or demanding parents; personal past histories that are sometimes so traumatic one wonders how the person has come through it all. These are the situations that are often brought up in the one-to-one sessions each week. They are too sensitive for group dissection (although people often do divulge the most staggering things in the group sessions; but that is only if they choose to, and never because they are pressured to do so). Or the person may just want to go over something again, wondering if she understands, or questioning it in her own circumstances.

And the one-to-ones give that opportunity for personal attention that is so important.

We are constantly reassessing the group format to make it as useful and meaningful as we possibly can. At the present time, this plan is working well and is well received. We always ask for feedback at the end of the series and often get very helpful comments.

There is an interesting phenomenon that we have seen in virtually every group. They start out on a terrific high, which lasts through the first two weeks. By the third week, they are drooping a little — no magic, you see. At somewhere around the sixth or seventh week, morale is at a very low level — once, we even had a mutiny, with letters from the group to us and some confrontative conversation! Then slowly, around week eight or nine, things start to pick up.

What has happened is that the group members have really begun to realize that the only way change is going to happen is if they decide that it *will* happen. By then, their self-esteem has also risen somewhat. They are taking a new look at themselves, and there is a little glimmer in that interior mirror that is pleasing to see.

We always warn the groups right at the beginning that this progression will happen. Then, when it does, we can reassure them that things are simply progressing normally.

But each group is different: one seems to really latch on to the metabolism aspect, another bunch focus determinedly on emotional factors. We just go with the flow.

19

Smokers' Program

The Smokers' Program is also given only in groups. We have elected to follow this concept because (a) it works better in groups and (b) it saves the patient money and the therapist time. (No, I do not have any statistics to back up "it works better in groups"—this is simply my clinical impression.)

The Smokers' group consists of four evening sessions, plus a booster six weeks later. Each session lasts about an hour.

During the four sessions, we deal with topics very similar to the weight program, although fewer:

Reward Systems
Helpful Gimmicks (Behavior Modification!)
Sabotage and Saboteurs; Patterns
Self-Hypnosis
What Your Lungs Look Like From the Inside (Ugh!)
Battle Plans for the Future

When discussing Reward Systems, we point out once again that old rewards were *valid when they began.* For instance, most people began smoking in their early teens and it had a great deal to do with peer pressure, wanting to appear sophisticated, etc. Those are very valid reasons at age 14. However, perhaps we could do without them when we're 40. Recognizing the old rewards, respecting them, and finishing with them is a useful thing to do. Then one can get on with elucidating the rewards of the present, which are often much more difficult to appreciate (even by the subject himself).

There is one reward which we point out to the group, especially to the women: fear of putting on weight if they stop is a reason for continuing to smoke.

The patterns are important because usually one can find some place to interrupt them other than by changing the smoking component, such as taking away the ashtray beside the telephone. Because the pattern has changed, the smoking aspect changes, too.

Health is the least important reason why people stop smoking. Everybody believes "it will never happen to me." Nevertheless, I go through the "What Your Lungs Look Like..." session because occasionally, someone is caught up by that and it makes an unexpected (by me) impact. Part of my patter is to tell them that "pools of pus" can gather where cavities have formed in the lung substance, a condition known as bronchiecstasis. One chap came out of hypnosis and in a dazed voice full of self-disgust said, "Pools of pus! Ugh!"—and he stopped smoking right then and there. Alas, he is the exception. I find it very hard to understand.

We do a lot of ego-strengthening throughout the series, and commend each member for his good efforts (no matter what the week has brought).

During Battle Plans for the Future, they visualize themselves dealing with situations where they would previously have always reached for a cigarette, and instead they are coping very well indeed. Usually, something to occupy the hands is useful; so is having a good process for dealing with saboteurs.

People respond to the group sessions in one of three ways. There is frequently one person in the group who stops smoking after the first session (even though no specific suggestion to do so is given); everybody hates him from then on (it is usually "him," for some reason) and HE KEEPS COMING!

There is frequently one person in the group who apparently makes no changes throughout the course. I will come back to that in a minute.

Most people make some definite—and sometimes drastic—changes throughout the four weeks, and are ready to give up those last three or four cigarettes a day when they come back for their booster session.

To those who seemingly have no change I say, "Take Heart. When you have taken care of whatever is getting in the way, whatever needs to be taken care of FIRST, then all the information is there for you, securely stored away in your subconscious mind, and it can be accessed and used just as effectively and perhaps even more so because of that clearing-away process."

There is always a lot of controversy as to whether it is better to quit "cold turkey" or gradually. I think this depends entirely on what each person wishes to do. We make no recommendations as to which is better, suggesting rather that they KNOW intuitively which approach will work best for them.

When they return for their six-week booster, we find about 70% have made significant changes in their smoking pattern; cutting down from three packs a day to three cigarettes a day is not uncommon. At that last session, most give up those last few.

I think part of the reason for our high success rate is that by the time they get around to coming to the group, it is The Court of Last Resort. They've "tried" everything else. They are ready to stop, and just need a bridge across that last canyon.

It always interests me how frequently someone will come up to me — on the street or in the supermarket, or drop in at the office or write a note, in order to tell me, "You were right. It finally clicked." The longest time lapse I have heard of was experienced by a patient in my own family practice who had taken the group with apparently no change. *Three years later,* I received a message via his mother-in-law (also a patient): "Tell Dr. Hunter that it finally clicked." That was two years ago, and he hasn't had a cigarette since.

On this same topic, I will always remember the oldest patient who ever came to one of the groups. She was 76. (I have had one or two older than that who came for individual hypnosis, but she was the oldest in a group.) She had been smoking three or more packs a day for over 60 years, and she came because she was going home to England to visit her 94-year-old mother, who did not approve of smoking.

A challenge!

She turned out to be one of those people who apparently made no changes throughout the four weeks, although her terrible stridorous breathing, which made me wonder if I was going to have to give CPR every time she came, seemed to ease a little.

Between the fourth session and the booster six weeks later, she had been to the U.K. for her month's holiday and was just back. She came into the room quite belligerently, glared at me and said, "Well, Dr. Hunter, I'm sorry to tell you that it didn't work at all, and I just had to quit by myself, Cold Turkey!"

At times we will receive a direct request for an authoritarian message. Someone wants me to say, "YOU WILL STOP SMOKING." We ordinarily shy away from such statements because we want to make sure the members in the group know that we are not responsible for their changes — THEY are responsible for their changes. However, I will sometimes accede to the request, prefacing it with, "You have asked me to give you this message, and so I give it to you on that understanding."

(Several times I have said "we" or "our"; sometimes I will lead the group, sometimes the psychologist does. We do not mix and match this group — I do all sessions or she does.)

About the groups in general: I give an information lecture once a month, in the office, about the groups we offer, their extent and duration, and the premises behind them. I want those who attend to know as much as possible about these basics before they even sign up for a group. I say to them, "You think you want to lose weight, or you want to quit smoking. You don't, you know. *(Great consternation!)* You would like to be slimmer, or you would like to be a nonsmoker; but that's different. You want to be through the process and out the other end. *(Reluctant nods of agreement.)* But you don't want to stop smoking, or you would have stopped. These groups are designed to help you find out why you are not doing what you think you want to do."

PART VIII

SEXUALITY

General Comments

Specific Techniques

20

General Comments

Because of its nature, sexual dysfunction is often difficult to resolve using conventional psychotherapeutic approaches. It is a very, very delicate subject, no matter how much people may deny that in this day and age.

For many, it is still an area where shame and guilt are rife, and it is not only older people who feel this way; it also applies to the young adults who are coping with changing mores, and are often in just as much trouble and are just as afraid to say so as their older fellow victims.

Frequently, the dysfunction began long before it was recognized, stemming from childhood confusions: overheard and mysterious conversations; strange sounds from behind the parents' bedroom door; perhaps even a soft scream—"OHHH!!" These are bewildering and very often frightening for children, who have no parameters with which to interpret them. And allusions to menstruation ("the curse"), wet dreams, and/or pregnancy by older brothers or sisters may add to the confusion.

Moreover, there is a tremendous emphasis these days on sexual performance. One must always be striving to measure up (as it were); to have bigger orgasms, longer orgasms, multi-orgasms, etc.

Making love is also a state of great vulnerability. Many feel (even if they cannot express it or do not consciously know it) that they have let down all their defenses when they have allowed someone, no matter how dear or caring or cared for that someone may be, to see them in the throes of a powerful sexual response. And because we are so vulnerable during the sexual experience, we may exaggerate the feelings, remarks, or attitude of the sexual partner.

Many of the above situations are relatively benign in themselves, but may have long-range effects. When one adds fearful or horrendous experiences, demoralizing early conditioning, and the onslaught of our media-focused society with its pervasive implications that one is somehow wrong or less than acceptable if his/her sexual life is different from what one reads about, the stage is set for an endless assortment of problems.

(Therapy for the soul-searing histories of child abuse is outside the scope of this manual. Some of the techniques are adaptable, but must be used in conjunction with psychotherapy and a wide variety of treatment modalities.)

Any tool that we use to help people with these problems must have unique qualities. Hypnosis is such a tool.

First and foremost, it gets away from the intellectualizing game. Nothing is more devastating to the nurturing of sexual response than analyzing it, dissecting it, and laying it out on the table (or the physician's desk) for inspection, examination, and assessment. Getting away from intellectualizing can also obviate the guilt-blame complex which is so common with these problems and allow the underlying anger to come through, where it can be acknowledged and dealt with.

We avoid the "yes-but" syndrome, both between patient and therapist and between one partner and the other. It allows the patient to put pride to one side, thus avoiding another huge pitfall. There are tremendous advantages in a tool that bypasses the intellectualizing game.

Second, it allows and is conducive to physical relaxation, at the time of discussion and therapy and also at the time of intercourse, which will certainly aid in achieving a natural, pleasant, and fulfilling response. Learning how to do this gives the patient a measure of control that he or she may otherwise feel is lacking.

Third, it allows the couple to obliterate YOU much more successfully, and therefore allows you to facilitate communication between THEM.

Fourth, it can be used both with individuals and with couples. A unique tool, indeed.

21

Specific Techniques

MUTUAL HYPNOSIS

Mutual hypnosis with couples (i.e., both parties are in hypnosis simultaneously) is very easy to do and extremely useful for getting through the barriers of embarrassment and difficulty people encounter in verbalizing about emotions.

Somehow, it facilitates the giving and receiving of messages, often messages so subtle that they are little understood even by those sending them. In hypnosis, neither partner need be on the defensive, and this is probably why the communication is so comparatively open.

The technique is simplicity itself. I usually have had at least one session individually with each, introducing him/her to what hypnosis is and how it is experienced. Then we schedule joint appointments for after office hours, when the office staff have gone and no one is in the waiting room. Usually, the couple stretch out on the floor — I have lots of pillows in the office. I sit on the floor also, between the two of them so that I can easily reach each person's forehead with my thumb. Luckily, I have two thumbs, and one comes slowly down to each forehead while I go through my usual induction patter.

When they are in hypnosis and feeling comfortable, I start with something relatively nonthreatening such as softly asking Mary to tell Jim about something that they do together — nonsexual — that she really enjoys. He then has a chance to respond to that and shares a similar pleasant enjoyment with her.

They are now feeling safer, and you can gradually ease them around to the agenda for the day — perhaps telling each other what he/she likes most about their sexual interaction, or an intimate happy memory. It seems to me that it works best when we save the things they do NOT like until several sessions later, when they are indeed reassured and have had enough ego-strengthening to be able to cope with that. Generally, focusing on what each enjoys or is thrilled by is more useful and certainly easier to accept than the other. The time comes, though,

though, when they ARE able to communicate their distresses in this very protected milieu.

Sometimes it is difficult to convince people that sexuality does not begin and end at the bedroom door. One of the most common complaints of the women is that the men just seem to expect them to drop the needle-pricks of the day and immediately feel interested in sex. This is the sort of message that they can begin to send and receive.

A useful technique, after they have had two or three sessions and are comfortable with the format, is to ask them to imagine themselves getting ready for bed, telling each other what they might be feeling as they are doing that:

She: I'm just getting undressed while he is in the bathroom . . .

He: I'm in the bathroom wondering if she is getting undressed, wondering why she doesn't want me to see her. She always seems to want to get undressed when I'm not around. I feel a little hurt. I like to look at her.

She: I think he must be turned off by the roll around my middle. I'm wondering if he's going to approach me. . . . *(silence)*

Dr.: *(very softly)* Do you want him to?

She: Yes, but I'm afraid that he isn't really interested, and just wants to do it and get it over with — he never seems to want to take much time.

He: I'm afraid that if I don't hurry up, she'll turn away.

Dr.: Tell her, Jim, how you are feeling.

He: I'm afraid that you'll turn away from me, so I go as fast as I can before you do.

She: But I need more time to feel closer to you, to get cuddled and kissed — you hardly ever kiss me anymore — do I smell bad?

He: No, of course not! You always smell wonderful, to me.

She: I need to be reassured that you really WANT me — ME, not just sex.

This sort of exchange can go on usefully for quite a long time, with the therapist gently guiding with soft questions or suggestions when necessary. Many times, the couple have told me that they were not even aware of where the questions came from — it just seemed to pop into their minds. The less we intervene, the better they can arrive at their own communicating.

After they come out of the hypnosis, the conversation may go like this:

He: Surely you don't think that I think you smell bad? *(This is not said disparagingly in any way, but in astonishment)*

She: Yes, I do — I worry about that a lot, because you seem to turn away from me so quickly when you've finished.

He: I'm usually thinking that you just want to go to sleep.

She: *(Shyly)* You used to let me go to sleep in your arms. I used to feel so loved. . . .

He: *(In disbelief)* But you know I love you!

This couple have begun to really communicate, perhaps for the first time in years. They may have said some of these same things to each other before, but in a confrontative, accusatory, or defensive way that closes off, rather than invites, communication.

The foregoing is a very simple little sketch, but it is fairly typical of how these sessions get started. From there, in future sessions, they can begin to give more detail about the explicit sexual difficulties. And some of these get very complicated, indeed.

Be sure you are very comfortable in your own sexuality. A couple may get into the thorny questions of infidelity and of sexual practices that seem unusual or distasteful to you, or each may want to entice you to his or her side. (STAY FIRMLY IN THE MIDDLE!) Are you at ease working with a homosexual couple? Would it be hard for you to stay neutral if one cross-dresses and the other finds this offensive or frightening?

If you feel twinges of a judgmental or biased response, you will do everyone a favor by referring them to someone else. The last thing a couple who are having sexual difficulties needs is to have us impose our rigidities on top of theirs.

A SAFE PLACE FOR THE CHILD TO STAY

(Note: This script is NOT suitable for a woman who has been sexually abused as a child. Child abuse is not a "misinterpretation." It could, perhaps, be adapted for use after there has been extensive and positive therapy concerning the abuse.)

Ease comfortably into hypnosis now, as I gently bring my thumb down to touch your forehead — you know exactly how to do that. That's right. And take yourself to whatever level is just right, to achieve what you're going to achieve today. Let me know by taking a very deep breath, when you have reached that best level.

"to achieve what you are going to achieve" presumes success

(It may take a little time for this to happen, because the topic is emotionally laden and your patient will want to make very sure that she feels "deep enough.")

Good. In our past few sessions, we have been exploring the sexual response and especially how YOU respond; and it has seemed to you as if there is something in the way, preventing you from feeling completely free to express your sexuality.

the potential for full response is there but is just somehow obstructed

It often happens that these interferences stem from the past—usually from childhood. Most commonly, they seem to arise from childhood misinterpretations or confusing—and therefore very frightening—experiences. So we are going to use your skills in hypnosis to review and reevaluate any such interferences from *your* childhood.

opportunity for reframing

Let your subconscious mind now take you backwards in time, to the time when some such event had taken or was taking place. That's right, just let it take you back to such a time. You may become aware of just what the situation was, or you may simply feel some very uncomfortable feelings—yes, I can see that you are experiencing some such feelings now—the feelings of that little girl. And she doesn't know what to do or what to make of that strange and perhaps frightening situation. She needs someone to help her.

regression to that earlier time

YOU can help her. Let the grown-up *(Margaret)* comfort little *(Peggy)*. That's right. *You* will know how to explain to her, perhaps in words or perhaps in some other way, in a way that she will be able to understand, that grown-ups sometimes do funny things that are hard to understand when you're still a little girl, but that is *alright*. Tell her that you know why she is upset, but it truly IS alright. Mummy is fine, she is safe in every way, and Daddy is okay, too.

adaptation of "comforting the child within" (p. 55)

But because it is so confusing when these
things happen, it would be a good idea to
find a very safe place for *(Peggy)* to stay at
these times. The two of you can collaborate
on finding or creating that safe place. Be
sure that it feels *very* safe to that little girl.

**how to prevent further
uncomfortable feelings**

(Give time for the creation of the safe place)

Have you found that safe place now? And
she feels REALLY safe there? Good.

Now you can explain to her — again, you will
know how to do this — that you are a grown-up
too, and sometimes YOU like to do some of
the things that seem so very confusing; but
from now on it will be much better because
whenever such things are about to happen,
you can just tell her to go to her very safe
place where she will be perfectly happy and
comfortable.

**find one's own inner
communication**

And she can stay there as long as she wishes —
perhaps until you go to sleep, or get up and
start doing something else that she
understands better.

This will take only a few seconds — just a very
brief word or thought directed to her — and
then you will know that she is safe, and that
you can fully explore and enjoy your own
sexuality.

**posthypnotic suggestion:
now the interference is
comfortably taken care of,
suggestion for successful
sexual experience**

Stay with her for a little longer. Then say
goodbye for now to that little girl, bring
yourself back to this present *(say the date),*
and so back into this room. Rest for a brief
time, then come out of your hypnosis in
your own way.

ERECTILE DYSFUNCTION

(The earlier part of the session has been spent on some other task: mind/body communication skills, stress management, back-to-before, etc.)

Before closing our session for today,
there are some important facts for you
to recognize.

You have a tremendous core of strength within you, and much information. Indeed, there is a strong, strong tower of information that can build up, gather together and build up from that strong, strong central core. And that tower of information builds and builds, and is always there for you. You can rely on that sturdy tower of strength. It is always there, waiting until you need it. Sturdy, strong, and reliable, a good solid core of information and strength, which comes from within you and is there for you, whenever you need it.

information can be experiential as well as intellectual

(For PREMATURE EJACULATION, you can add something like this:)

And that tower of strength will stay there
until you need it, stay strong and sturdy until
you call for it.

It's wonderful to know that you have those
resources, waiting until you need them,
strong and virile within you.

(The above are good examples of how blatantly and outrageously we can manipulate language, once the critical evaluation of the conscious mind is put aside. I am always astonished that it works at all, but in fact it works very well indeed.)

ROLE REVERSAL

Role Reversal is a specific variation of Mutual Hypnosis.

It is an extremely powerful technique, very evocative and highly emotional. It is an approach to be used only after the couple have had the opportunity to experience hypnosis, and preferably mutual hypnosis, several times.

I shall describe it with a case history.

Mr. and Mrs. K. have been married for over 20 years. They are a truly loving couple, with excellent communication. There are four children, aged 20 to 14. The 18-year-old girl is mentally retarded, with a functional age of about eight years, so there are problems of privacy and concern about the future.

Mrs. B.K. has always had difficulty achieving orgasm, although she has good libido. The good libido is a mixed blessing, because she wishes so desperately for orgasmic fulfillment. This situation had become very distressing for them both, and on their request they were referred for possible hypnosis.

Mrs. B.K. came from a strongly Puritan family, where "fleshly matters" were never discussed. One childhood memory is of being in the bath and, when washing her genitalia, being told to "scrub the dirty parts very hard." Mr. R.K., on the other hand, came from an easygoing family where any topic was acceptable for open discussion.

The couple had had several hypnosis sessions, individually and as a couple, before I broached the possibility of using role reversal. I spent considerable time discussing what that meant, and they agreed that it could perhaps break through what seemed to be a stalemate in therapy.

Once they were in hypnosis (as described on page 191), I requested that Brenda temporarily become Richard and Richard become Brenda. Then I asked them to describe what they were feeling as they prepared for bed. When I asked Richard to answer, Brenda's voice replied, "I'm wondering if she'll turn off again tonight."

The session progressed in this way, each answering *what she/he perceived the other to be feeling.* When it came time to end the session, I asked them to resume their usual identities, then come out of hypnosis in their own way. Brenda returned first, obviously wanting to avoid questions for a little while; but Richard took a long, long time to come out of hypnosis. When he finally did, tears were coursing down his face. "I thought I understood her pain," he said, "but I never knew how terrible it really is."

There has been no magic answer for this couple, but the situation is less tense. Richard found that he wanted to be even more gentle and patient in his lovemaking. He had "heard" her when, during that hypnosis, she had said (as Richard), "I wish she'd come so that I could get relief." On the other hand, Brenda "heard" when he said (as Brenda), "He only wants to get this over with — I'm just dragging him back."

That is one of the great values of the role-reversal technique: misconceptions about what the partner is thinking or feeling become very evident and can then later be discussed and clarified.

Because the hypnotic experience involves interaction on an intensely emotional level, open discussion is often highly charged after they come out of their hypnosis. Go softly until they have time to gather their wits together. I usually leave the room for a few minutes so that they can embrace, before offering a few comments and the suggestion to go home and keep the communication flowing.

CHANGES IN SELF-IMAGE

Sometimes a change in status will subsequently create changes in self-image that intrude upon the natural expression of sexuality. This may account for the frequency with which "sex was wonderful until we were married — and then it just started getting less and less satisfying."

The root of the decreased libido may well lie in the change of status. One young woman who professed the above "sex was wonderful . . ." situation told me, in an offhand way, that lots of things were different since she'd had the baby. For instance, she had come across a pair of frivolous sandals in her cupboard, so of course she had had to put them away, but she felt a little sad that she wouldn't be wearing them any more. "Whoa!" said I. "What is THAT all about?"

"Well, of course I can't wear them any more," she responded. "I mean, I'm a *mother,* now."

Due to a complicated convolution of interpretations(!) that doubtless involved her own mother, she had believed that being a mother meant that you "put away frivolous things." This apparently included sexual enjoyment — not appropriate for a mother!

Hypnotic intervention was very straightforward, reinterpreting her role definitions, restoring her sense of self and rehearsing success. She did very well indeed.

There are also changes in body image after childbirth or surgery that can interfere greatly with sexual expression. Aging, or fear of aging, may bring similar problems for some people (male or female). These concepts, involving so much emotional content, are much more accessible through hypnosis than through cognitive therapy. I use back-to-before, into-the-future, role reversal, dissociation (to "see" from a different perspective), and a lot of ego-strengthening techniques.

PART IX

REHABILITATION

General Concepts

Research

Techniques

22

General Concepts

The use of hypnotic techniques to aid in rehabilitation is only just beginning to be explored. With the burgeoning interest in mind/body healing, however, it certainly makes sense. And because there is usually such an overwhelming emotional component, the hypnotic approach may turn out to be the most rewarding.

We know that the greater the emotional investment, the greater the chance of success using the opportunities offered by altered states of consciousness. Just think of miracle healers, Lourdes, and the like.

The term "Rehabilitation" is broad, and can mean recovery from a heart attack, a severe motor vehicle accident, or a stroke, to name just a few. There has been increasing research into the use of hypnosis in these cases, which were previously considered out of the realm of such interventions (see Research and References).

It is certainly time we began to utilize our own talents more fruitfully in this still-neglected field. Who knows? Perhaps we may help spawn a miracle or two.

23

Research

In a recent paper, Harris, Porges et al. (1993), using the Harvard Group Scale of Hypnotic Susceptibility, demonstrated that autonomic tone, as assessed by cardiac vagal tone and heart rate reactivity, are measurably related to hypnotic susceptibility. This has immense importance for the use of hypnosis in cardiac rehabilitation — especially when we consider Felten's work (1993) in psychoneuro-immunology and the impact of some stress hormones on some brain cells.

It doesn't take much of a leap to start considering the role of hypnosis in ALL post-cardiac patients.

Spellacy (1991) reports on the types of hypnotic interventions to which brain-damaged patients respond. He feels that there is a major role for hypnosis in such cases, previously considered unapproachable, if we are cognizant of their special needs.

And Pajntar, Rudel and Roskar (1989) reported on their EMG study of muscle fatigue in hypnosis at the Fourth European Congress in Oxford in 1987, published in the 1989 Proceedings of that meeting. One presumes there will be further work with regard to hypnotic interventions in post-traumatic cases where there has been muscle/nerve damage causing muscle weakness.

This is just a tiny sampling of the work that is being done in the rehabilitation field.

24

Techniques

YOU ALREADY HAVE THE INFORMATION

Most of the hypnotic approaches to rehabilitation that I use are based on the assumption that somewhere in the brain the subject already has the information stored that he/she needs; that it is accessible through hypnosis; and that it can be put to use in these new circumstances.

The bridge between the first and third of these premises—that this information is accessible through hypnosis—may be a great leap in trance logic on my part, but it makes perfect sense to the subject and offers that one vital ingredient which so many rehabilitation programs lack: a new opportunity, a chance to break out of the soul-eroding cycle of "trying" the same thing over and over again to the point of exhausted surrender.

One is STILL doing the same thing (i.e., physio, exercise, speech therapy), but the new emphasis gives back to it a dimension of adventure.

And that can make all the difference.

TEACHING THE OTHER SIDE OF THE BRAIN

You know that you have been able to perform many functions throughout your life—things like walking and talking and writing and feeding yourself. These became second nature to you many many years ago.

you already have the information

Then, three months ago when you had your stroke, you found that very suddenly you

calmly stating the fact

205

were unable to do those very things that
you have done automatically for decades.

So the past three months have been very
confusing and difficult, because of this strange
and frustrating situation. In particular, you   **acknowledging the**
have had a hard time speaking, because you   **feelings, reassuring that**
seem to lose the words that you are looking   **they are normal**
for. This has been all the more exasperating
and depressing because you have always been
so articulate.

Your doctor has explained that the stroke
affected the left side of your brain, the side
where the speech center is located. That is
why you are having trouble with your words.   **opening up another**
However, the *right* side of your brain is fine.   **possibilty**

Here is an interesting challenge for you,   **often they are longing for**
then — *teach the right side of your brain to do*   **a dramatic approach —**
what the left side used to do!   **here is one**

This will be all the more interesting because
the right side of the brain seems to be more
active in the realm of imagery, music, and
creativity, even though we know that both   **crossover**
sides of the brain can perform all the various
functions, and there is a tremendous crossover
in activity.

But this is just what you need! Think of the   **spoken very gently,**
possibilities — the right side of the brain has all   **but very intensely**
the potential that it needs to learn the various
speech functions, and it has great powers of   **affirming the validity of**
creativity, too!   **this approach; the right**
    side *specially* designed for
    such a challenge

Because brain activity is physiological as well
as mental, you will also need to focus very
determinedly on mind/body communication.
All the information about biochemistry and

neurophysiology must be fully accessible to
your subconscious mind, and the information
that the subconscious holds must be accessible
to the body.

So, ask your subconscious mind and your
body to get into strong communication, in
order to cooperate and collaborate fully in
this venture.

The project, then, is this: the left side of your
brain must teach the right side of your brain
what to do in order for you to find the words
you want and speak clearly and freely again.

**restating the original
suggestion in a new way:
inner learning through
inner teaching**

Did you know that you have a bridge from one
side of your brain to the other? You have. It is
called the corpus callosum. It is a very strong
bridge connecting the two hemispheres of the
brain. How wonderful that you have a bridge
already there! It can be one of the routes that
information can take as it is transferred from
the left side to the right.

**the concept of a bridge is
reassuring — bridges ARE
transportation routes**

In your own way, create the image of this
bridge in your mind, and envision or feel or
hear or have the very strongest sense of information travelling across this bridge, from the
left side of the brain, to the right.

**combining fact and
imagery**

When it gets to the right side, let it find the
exact place to settle — somewhere accessible,
where other information coming in can find
it easily and add to it.

"right side" is symbolic

Then, when the information is safely lodged
in the right side of the brain, again invoke that
wonderful mind/body communication as you
direct your right brain to *begin to use that
information!* You can be very, very curious

presumption of success

about how that will happen. Will you feel like
speaking, and find that some promising sound
comes forth? Will you say it all in your mind
first, and then find the way to make your
mouth and tongue work properly? How will
it come about?

We know that this will probably take a very
concerted effort over some period of time —
after all, it took you some period of time to
learn how to speak in the first place, so it is
reasonable that it will take some time for your
right brain to learn to do what your left brain
has been doing.

preparing for a long effort

Stay patient, then — in the long run, this will
be the shorter way. Stay patient and calm, and
let the left side of your brain teach the right
side what to do.

mildly confusing statement

Remember, too, that there are other ways of
transferring information besides sending it
across a bridge. Send that information to catch
a ride on a passing hormone, for instance.
There is great hormone involvement in any
learning process. This is another opportunity
for mind/body communication and
collaboration.

more creative imagery

And then there will be possibilities that
only the deepest part of your subconscious
mind knows about or has access to; so, in
your own hypnosis every day, remember
to ask your subconscious to use ALL the
information that it has, to help you in this
challenging project.

covering all bases

**several words with
multilevels of meaning
are reiterated throughout,
e.g., bridge, cross-over,
creativity, "right side"**

You know more than you know that you
know. And learning what you already know
is a wonderful experience.

**a good old Ericksonian
comment**

**"learning what you already
know" — hypnotic language**

ONCE LEARNED, CAN BE RE-LEARNED

Today I'm going to talk about learning.

But I'm going to talk about it in a rather different way. I'm going to talk about learning how to do *something you already know how to do!*

catching attention with unusual statement

When you were very small, just a baby boy *(girl)*, you had to learn how to walk; to get yourself up on your feet, standing straight, putting one foot ahead of the other, and taking steps to get yourself to somewhere else from where you were.

setting the background for the statement

Your conscious mind hasn't thought about that for decades. Walking came to be such an automatic thing, thinking about it was entirely unnecessary. Your subconscious mind recognized, "I want to go over *there*. . . ," your body took over, and you went.

However, a lot of learning — of trial and error, of finding out about the relationship of objects to other objects and, most of all, of motor skills — was dedicated to learning to walk for quite a long time before you were able to walk steadily and safely, to stop and start just when you wanted to, and to go in the precise direction that you wanted to go.

invitation to realize all the ingredients

Over the years, you have walked and walked and walked. Your body and your brain and your mind have collaborated so often on that activity called walking that you know all there is to know about it. You even know how to walk backwards!

mind/body communication exemplified

curious ability!

Six months ago a sudden, confusing, and distressing thing happened to you: you had a stroke. And that stroke affected the particular part of your brain that was involved in walking.

acknowledging fact

Now your muscles apparently refuse to do
what you tell them to do, and they are weak
and flabby. You have been going to physiotherapy diligently to regain your muscle
strength in your legs and arms.

**reassuring that he has
been doing his best**

Yet, your feet and ankles and knees and hips
are still obstinately staying put instead of
going where you want them to go.

recognizing frustration

This has been very frustrating; and you know
from some of our previous sessions, when we find
something to be very frustrating, that indicates
that we must look for a different approach.

**a problem is an
opportunity to do
something different**

Let us explore, then, a new avenue. We can
do that by putting the whole situation into a
new framework.

reframing

When you were a baby, you learned how to do
something you had not done before. Then how
about — *again learning to do it!*

the invitation

Now, THAT makes sense. After all, if you
can learn how to do it once (and when you
were just a baby, at that), you can learn how
to do it again when you have *all that previous
experience about learning.*

**reflecting the opening
statement**

Yes. You have already learned how to learn
how to walk. Therefore, you can relearn what
you already have learned, calling on your
subconscious to search out that previous
learning and learn to put it to new use.

**"learned how to learn
how to . . ." — hypnotic
emphasis and further
emphasizes the "learn"
throughout the script**

In order to do that searching, go further into
hypnosis now. Use my thumb as a focusing
point, and go "way down" into hypnosis, as far
as you need to go to achieve what you need to
achieve. That's right. Good.

*(placing my thumb on
his forehead again —
deepening)*

Now, let your subconscious mind go back
to the time when you were a small baby, just   **regression**
learning how to walk. Go back to the beginning
of those lessons — and that beginning may even
have been before you were born, when you
were experiencing what it was like to move
within the ocean of the amniotic fluid. Ask
your subconscious mind to REVIEW ALL
THAT LEARNING, and find out what you
need to know again, as you relearn what you   **further emphasis, referring**
have already learned so many years ago.   **to earlier phrases**

Feel again what it is like to learn how to walk.
Let all your senses be clear as you reexperience
that — the muscle tone, the awareness of some-   **kinesthetic imagery**
thing that you would later call strength, and
the sense of position and of how you know
your feet are on the ground; the exquisitely
complicated movement of the foot as it lifts in
a step and swings forward — all there for your
subconscious mind and your body, together,
to review and reexplore.

Ask your subconscious mind to review all that
old information many times a day, for as many
days as it needs to, and then to *redirect that*   **the information is needed**
information to the present.   **NOW**

At the same time as your subconscious mind
is "re- viewing" that previous learning, you are
regaining muscle strength through your therapy,
so that soon the two approaches can merge,   **more mind/body**
and you will begin to learn again what you   **communication**
have already known for many decades.

Once learned, skills can be relearned.   **reinforcement**

This new approach calls for the greater possible collaboration between mind (conscious
and subconscious) and body. Reinforce that

collaboration every day in your own hypnosis, reminding yourself that you already know what you are now learning, and you are putting that knowledge to good use as you approach this worthwhile endeavor in this renewed and worthwhile way.

> **"you already know what you are learning"— referring again to opening statement**

(This same approach can be used for those who have become aphasic; once language has been learned, it can be relearned; once one has learned, as a very small child, how to speak, one can relearn, etc. This approach and the previous one can also be effectively combined.)

OTHER APPROACHES

The "Train Station" metaphor described on page 167 *(Children — Learning Disabilities)* is quite adaptable to post-CVA rehabilitation, both for speech problems and also for relearning motor skills.

Also in the case of post-stroke amnesia, some of the *Memory-Enhancement* techniques may be useful (p. 138).

The *Progressive-Retrogressive* technique (p. 114) may be adaptable. Or one can *Rehearse Success,* especially with regard to regaining motor function and speech. The key is to rehearse in incredible detail, stressing the coordination needed in even the simplest movement.

Use LOTS of ego-strengthening!! Be realistically positive.

Research and References

Ader, R., see Moyers, B.D., *Healing and the Mind,* pp. 239–256.

    Dr. Ader describes his landmark experiment showing that one could establish a psychological conditioned response in mice by first giving them sugar water containing a cytotoxic drug, and then producing continuing response, as if to that drug, using only the sugar water, so that the mice died because the mouse-mind *thought* it was still receiving the cytotoxic drug.

Barber, J. Rapid induction analgesia: A clinical report. *American Journal of Clinical Hypnosis, 17.* 1977, pp. 138–147.

Beares, J.O. Hypnotic transactions, and the evolution of psychological structure. In Hall, R.C.W. and Torem, M. (Eds): *Psychiatric Medicine.* Vol. 10, No. 1. Ryandic Publishing, Longwood, FL, 1992, pp. 25–39.

    This paper explores the interaction of hypnotic transactions and psychological structure. It addresses the questions of "differential responsibility," of the "nature of psychological structure," and some of the clinical and forensic dilemmas inherent in the field today.

Ebrahim, D.W. Neurolinguistic programming — an 'alternative' British perspective. *Hypnos, XV, 2:* pp. 93–99. (HYPNOS is the Journal of the Swedish Society of Clinical and Experimental Hypnosis)

    In this paper, Dr. Ebrahim discusses the differences of his model from the classical neurolinguistic programming (NLP) definition as presented by Michael Heap in 1988, and the applicability of NLP as an adjunctive "alternative therapy." He also presents a graphic depiction of the NLP concept.

    Dr. Ebrahim (personal communication) emphasized that ". . . the technology of NLP, in the main, is derived from the concepts of Milton Erickson." In his own work as a psychotherapist he has chosen some ". . . very elegant techniques for the translation of insight into action — elegant inasmuch (as) they reflect the admirable qualities of the Master himself."

Evans, F.J. The hypnotizable patient. In *Hypnosis: The Fourth European Congress at Oxford.* Waxman, D., et al. (Eds). Whurr Publishers, London, 1989.

Felten, D., see Moyers, B.D. *Healing and the Mind,* pp. 213–237.

    Dr. Felton and his wife identified the nerve fibers that physically link the immune system with the nervous system. He describes the state of the art in psychoneuroimmunology.

Ferreiro, O. Hypnosis: Its use in acute attacks of bronchial asthma. (1993, *xx*, 4; *Hypnos:* pp. 236–245.)

This work was first submitted ". . . towards the title of Specialist, First Grade, in Allergy." Havana, Cuba. 1986.

Gillett, C.A., Griffiths, M.D. & Davies, P. The hypnotic suppression of conditioned electrodermal responses. In Waxman, D., et al. (Eds): *Hypnosis: The Fourth European Congress at Oxford.* Whurr Publishers, London, 1989.

This paper is interesting because it contradicts previous findings that neutral hypnosis does not influence conditioned electrodermal response, and also refutes Pavlov's theory of hypnosis and conditioning. This type of research is invaluable — it forces us to continuously reexamine our previous mind-sets.

Goleman, D. Wounds that never heal. *Psychology Today,* 1992. *Jan–Feb.* pp. 63–66 (concluded on p. 88).

As part of the ongoing research into how memories are processed and encoded, recently much attention has been paid to traumatic memory and its sequelae. Rather than "remember" these events, victims are catapulted back, in a kind of mental time-warp, *to the event.* It is just as if it were happening again, with all the hormonal, biochemical, and physiological responses that were aroused at the initial trauma. The research indicates that people must learn how to cope with these disturbing reenactments, rather than expect to be "cured" of the reactions.

Harris, R.M., et al. Hypnotic susceptibility, mood state, and cardiovascular reactivity. *American Journal of Clinical Hypnosis,* 1993, *36, 1;* pp. 15–25.

This paper explores the relationship between hypnotic susceptibility and cardiovascular parameters — blood pressure, heart rate, and cardiac vagal tone. The authors found that ". . . subjects with lower heart rate and greater vagal tone during baseline and greater heart rate increases during mood induction were more susceptible to hypnosis." They used the Harvard Group Scale of Hypnotic Susceptibility for their measurements of hypnotizability.

Hunter, M.E. Dissociative techniques in pain relief and pain relief in dissociative disorders. *Hypnos, XVI, 3* 1989; pp. 134–139.

Katz, J. Psychophysical correlates of phantom limb experience. *Journal of Neurology. Neurosurgery and Psychiatry,* 1992, *55, 9:* pp. 811–821.

This paper lays the groundwork for the following paper below. It is quite technical. Katz says: "The results of the study agree with recent suggestions that phantom limb pain is not a unitary syndrome, but a symptom class with each class subserved by different aetiological mechanisms," and goes on to refer to earlier work with Melzack in which ". . . a class of phantom limb pain which resembles in quality and location a pain experienced in the limb before amputation. Although the precise physiological mechanisms that underlie these somatosensory pain memories are unknown, the presense of pre-amputation pain clearly is a necessary condition for these phantom pains to develop."

Katz, J. Psychophysiological contributions to phantom limbs. *Canadian Journal of Psychiatry,* 1993, *37, 5:* pp. 282–298.

> According to Dr. Katz, the data offer strong further indication that pain that is experienced prior to amputation may persist in the form of a somatosensory memory in the phantom limb. He discusses input from the sympathetic nervous system, psychological and emotional factors, and what he describes as somato-sensory reorganization. These studies have important implications for anyone working with pain, especially chronic pain syndromes, and with abuse and trauma survivors.

Kemeny, M., see Moyers, B.D., *Healing and the Mind,* pp. 195–212.

> In his research protocol, Dr. Kemeny uses actors to explore whether emotions which are experienced over a period of, for example, 20 minutes affect the immune system. The data suggest that any emotion produces effects on the immune system, which in turn affect the body in a positive or negative way.

Matheson, G., Shue, K.L. Hypnotic language: A study of the experience of direct vs. indirect hypnosis. In Waxman, D., et al. (Eds.) *Hypnosis: The Fourth European Congress at Oxford.* Whurr Publishers, London, 1989.

Melzak, R., Wall, P.D. Pain mechanisms: A new theory. *Science, 150:* 1965. pp. 971–979.

Miller, S.C., Triggiano, P.T. The psychophysiological investigation of multiple person-ality disorder: Review and update. *American Journal of Clinical Hypnosis,* 1992, 35, 1; pp. 47–61.

> This is an exceptionally thorough review paper of data presented in the literature and at professional conferences on dissociative disorders. Although it addresses these conditions specifically, because of the nature of dissociation, it has implications for all hypnotic work. The research into dissociative disorders has opened up immense new insights into mind-body communication.

Moyers, B.D. *Healing and the Mind.* Doubleday, New York, 1993.

> This book contains the transcripts of the Public Television series of the same name and deserves to be on the shelf of every person who is interested in the mind/body connection. Of particular interest are the interviews with Candace Pert, Ph.D., David Felton, M.D., Ph.D., Robert Ader, Ph.D., Karen Olness, M.D., David Spiegel, M.D., and Margaret Kemeny, Ph.D.

> Above all, the message from these eminent clinicians and researchers is that mind and body are the same, a unity. It is impossible to separate them and therefore we should start speaking and thinking of "mind-body" rather than "mind and body."

Olness, K., see Moyers, B.D., *Healing and the Mind,* pp. 71–85.

> Dr. Olness describes a case history of a child with debilitating migraine headaches who learned to relieve them herself using biofeedback techniques, and another case history of a child with lupus erythematosis who had had to be maintained on incredibly high doses of steroids and was able to wean herself off them using techniques similar to those described by Robert Ader.

Pajntar, M., Rudel, D., Roskar, E. EMG study of muscle fatigue in hypnosis. In Waxman, D., et al. (Eds):*Hypnosis: The Fourth European Congress at Oxford.* Whurr Publishers, London, 1989.

This paper presented evidence that supported previous studies, viz. that hypnosis exerts an influence on the onset of muscle fatigue. Their spectral frequency analyses ". . .show that different suggestions in hypnosis play a role not only in motivation but very probably also in supraspinal stimulation or destimulation of recruiting the contraction of individual muscle fibers."

Pert, C., see Moyers, B.D., *Healing and the Mind,* pp. 177–194.

Dr. Pert describes her research with neuropeptides, the chemical messengers linking mind and body. She calls these neuropeptides "biochemical units of emotion." This is work of which all who work in the field of hypnosis and psychosomatic medicine need to be aware, and she describes it clearly in language that everyone can understand.

Robinson, L., et al. Behavioural techniques in psychophysiological insomnia. *British Columbia Medical Journal,* 1993, *33, 6:* pp. 351–353.

Ms. Robinson and her colleagues discuss the improved outcome of behavioural techniques, rather than medication, for effective sleep management. They address sleep hygiene, relaxation and biofeedback training, cognitive treatments, stimulus control, and sleep restriction. They say, "Progressive relaxation is foremost among those treatments that attempt to influence sleep by modifying the quality of preceding wakeful periods."

Rossi, E.L. *The Psychobiology of Mind-Body Healing.* W.W. Norton & Co., Inc., New York, 1986.

This important work outlines the state-dependent learning theory, postulating the pathways of mind-body communication, especially the limbic-hypothalamic-pituitary axis. He states: "State-dependent memory, learning and behaviour phenomena are the "missing link" in all previous theories of mind-body relationships. They bridge the mysterious gap between mind and body. . . ." Further: "All methods of mind-body healing and therapeutic hypnosis operate by accessing and reframing the state-dependent memory and learning systems that encode symptoms and problems," (p. 55).

Rossi, E.L., Cheek, D.B. *Mind-Body Therapy;* W.W. Norton & Co., Inc., New York, 1988.

This work extends the previous book by Rossi; he has taken many of the published papers by Cheek and added theoretical introductions and suggestions for 64 research projects. It is full of practical suggestions for applying hypnosis to many medical and surgical situations.

Schoen, M. Resistance to health: When the mind interferes with the desire to become well. *American Journal of Clinial Hypnosis,* 1993, *36,1:* pp. 47–53.

Secondary gain has not been appropriately evaluated with regard to its impact on such diseases as cancer or autoimmune disease, Dr. Schoen believes. In his paper he discusses how such secondary gain can result in "resistance to health" and create, e.g., medical noncompliance. Hypnosis is a useful tool for uncovering such resistance and therefore offers opportunity for addressing it directly.

Smith, M.R. The problem of apparent parasympathetic relaxation. Paper presented at the 9th International Conference on Multiple Personality/Dissociative States, Chicago, 1992.

    This paper "...focuses on the loss of the usual regulatory function of the autonomic nervous system in persons with chronic trauma-induced dissociation.... This phenomemon has important implications for treatment...[the therapist] may believe an apparently relaxed client is actually relaxed rather than in a state of hyper-repression." The implications are also valid for other work in hypnosis when we are dealing with an agitated client.

Spellacy, F. Hypnotherapy following traumatic brain injuries. *Hypnos, XVIX* (sic) *1:* 1992, pp. 34–39.

    Dr. Spellacy explains that people who have sustained traumatic brain injuries may have cognitive deficits that make it difficult for them to profit from the usual psycho-therapeutic approaches which, he points out, "rely heavily on discursive language, effortful problem solving and insight." On the contrary, he feels that hypnotherapeutic techniques are well suited for use with such patients.

Spiegel, D., see Moyers, B.D., *Healing and the Mind,* 1993, pp. 157–176.

    Dr. Spiegel has published widely on the subjects of pain, the clinical uses of hyp-nosis, and the psychosocial effects of support systems. This interview describes his study, originally published in *Lancet,* of controlled groups of women with metastatic breast cancer; one group had the support group added to the protocol—otherwise, they were evenly matched. The women in the support group had a remarkably improved outcome, much better than expected and much better than the women in the other group. He also describes the use of self-hypnosis in such regimes.

Spiegel, H., Greenleaf, M. Personality style and hypnotizability: The Fix-Flex con-tinuum. In Hall, R.C.W. & Torem, M. (Eds.): *Psychiatric Medicine,* Ryandic Pub-lishing, Longwood, FL, *Vol 10, No.1.* 1992, pp. 13–24.

    This paper, co-authored by one of the original proponents of the Hypnotic Induction Profile (HIP) (Spiegel), proposes that the HIP offers the technology required to "...identify which aspects of the person are relatively fixed (ecologically insensitive) and which aspects are relatively malleable (ecologically sensitive)." They refer to this as the Fix-Flex continuum, and believe that it is instrumental in predicting treatment responsivity.

Wyke, B. Neurophysiology and hypnosis. In Hunter, M.E. (Ed): *Frontiers of Hypnosis.* SeaWalk Press, West Vancouver, B.C. 1987, pp. 1–16.

    Professor Wyke, in the lead plenary session of the 1st National Assembly of the Federation of Canadian Societies of Clinical Hypnosis, states his theme: "What I am proposing to you is that in terms of our understanding of contemporary behavioural neurology, hypnosis can be regarded as a state of modified attention, created by modifications brought about in the central nervous system, by external or internal stimuli...."

Bibliography

Ader, R. (Ed). *Psychoneuroimmunology.* Academic Press, New York, 1981.

Antonovsky, A. *Health, Stress and Coping.* Jossy-Bass Publishers, San Francisco CA, 1980.

Bandler, R., Grinder, J. *Frogs into Princes: Neuro-Linguistic Programming.* Real People Press, Moab, Utah, 1979.

Bandler, R., Grinder, J. *Reframing: Neuro-Linguistic Programming and the Transformation of Meaning.* Real People Press, Moab, Utah, 1982.

Barber, J., Adrian, C. (Eds). *Psychological Approaches to the Management of Pain.* Brunner/Mazel, Publishers, New York, 1982.

Barnett, E. *Analytical Hypnotherapy, Principles and Practice.* Junica Publishing, Kingston, Ontario, 1981.

Borysenko, J. *Minding the Body, Mending the Mind.* Addison-Wesley Publishing Co., Reading, Massachusetts, 1987.

Cheek, D.B., LeCron, L.M. *Clinical Hypnotherapy.* Grune and Stratton, Inc., New York, 1968.

Crasilneck, H.B., Hall, J.A. *Clinical Hypnosis, Principles and Applications*, 2nd Ed. Grune and Stratton Inc., Orlando, FL, 1985.

De Bono, E. *PO: Beyond Yes and No.* Pelican Books, Harmondsworth, England, 1973.

De Bono, E. *Practical Thinking.* Pelican Books, Harmondsworth, England, 1976.

Donoghue, P.J., Siegel, M.E. *Sick and Tired of Feeling Sick and Tired.* W.W. Norton & Co., New York, 1992.

Frank, J.D. *Persuasion and Healing.* Schocken Books, New York, 1974.

Gardner, G.G., Olness, K. *Hypnosis and Hypnotherapy with Children.* Grune and Stratton Inc., New York, 1981.

Grinder, J., Bandler, R. *The Structure of Magic II.* Science and Behavior Books, Inc., Palo Alto, CA, 1976.

Hall, R.C.W., Torem, M. (Eds). *Psychiatric Medicine: Hypnosis and Its Clinical Application in Psychiatry and Medicine.* Vol. 10, No. 1, Ryandic Publishing, Inc., Longwood, FL, 1992.

Hammond, D.C. (Ed). *Handbook of Hypnotic Suggestions and Metaphors.* W.W. Norton & Co., New York, 1990.

Hanson, P.G. *The Joy of Stress.* Hanson Stress Management Organization, Islington, Ontario, 1985.

Hilgard, R.H., Hilgard, J.R. *Hypnosis in the Relief of Pain.* Wm. Kauffman, Inc., Los Altos, CA, 1975.

Hunter, M.E. *Psych Yourself in: Hypnosis and Health.* SeaWalk Press, Ltd., West Vancouver, BC, 1984, 1987.

Hunter, M.E. (Ed). *Frontiers of Hypnosis* (Proceedings of the 1st National Assembly, Federation of Canadian Societies of Clinical Hypnosis). SeaWalk Press, Ltd., West Vancouver, BC, 1986.

Jeffers, S. *Feel the Fear and Do It Anyway.* Fawcett Columbine, New York, 1987.

Jevne, R.F. *It All Begins with Hope: Patients, Caregivers & the Bereaved Speak Out.* LuraMedia, San Diego, 1991.

Jevne, R.F., Levitan, A. *No Time for Nonsense: Self-Help for the Seriously Ill.* LuraMedia, San Diego, 1989.

Lynch, J.J. *The Broken Heart: The Medical Consequences of Loneliness.* Basic Books, Inc., New York, 1977.

Moyers, B.D. *Healing and the Mind.* Doubleday, New York, 1993.

Pulos, L. *Beyond Hypnosis.* Omega Press, Vancouver, Canada, 1990.

Rose, L. *Overcoming Pain.* McCulloch Publishing Pty Ltd., Carlton, Victoria, Australia, 1990.

Rossi, E.L. *The Psychobiology of Mind-Body Healing.* W.W. Norton & Co., New York, 1986.

Rossi, E.L., Cheek, D.B. *Mind-Body Therapy: Methods of Ideodynamic Healing in Hypnosis.* W.W. Norton & Co., New York, 1988.

Shor, R.E., Orne, E.C. *Harvard Group Scale of Hypnotic Susceptibility. Form A.* Consulting Psychologists Press, Palo Alto, 1962.

Siegel, B.S. *Love, Medicine & Miracles.* Harper & Row, New York, 1988.

Waxman, D., Pedersen, D., Wilkie, I., Mellett, P. (Eds). *Hypnosis: The Fourth European Congress at Oxford.* Whurr Publishers, London, 1989.

Weitzenhoffer, A.M., Hilgard, E.R. *Stanford Hypnotic Susceptibility Scale. Form C.* Consulting Psychologists Press, Palo Alto, 1962.

Wester, W.C. (Ed). *Clinical Hypnosis: A Case Management Approach.* Behavioral Science Centre Inc. Publications, Cincinnati, 1987.